Management
of Organizational
Behavior

Utilizing Human Resources

PAUL HERSEY / KENNETH H. BLANCHARD

Ohio University, Athens, Ohio

Management of Organizational Behavior

Utilizing Human Resources

Prentice-Hall, Inc., Englewood Cliffs, New Jersey

C-13-548669-6
P-13-548644-0
Library of Congress Catalog Card Number: 76-84749
Current printing (last number)
10 9 8 7 6 5 4 3

PRENTICE-HALL INTERNATIONAL, INC., *London*
PRENTICE-HALL OF AUSTRALIA PTY. LTD., *Sydney*
PRENTICE-HALL OF CANADA, LTD., *Toronto*
PRENTICE-HALL OF INDIA, PRIVATE LTD., *New Delhi*
PRENTICE-HALL OF JAPAN, INC., *Tokyo*

Printed in the United States of America

To Our Parents

Preface

For a long time management theory has been characterized by a search for universals—a preoccupation with discovering essential elements of all organizations. The discovering of common elements is necessary, but they do not really provide practitioners with "principles" that can be applied with universal success.

In the past decade there has appeared a relative maturity in this field as it begins to focus on "patterned variations"—situational differences. We assume that there are common elements in all organizations, but we also assume differences among them and in particular the managing of their human resources. As the inventory of empirical studies expands, making comparisons and contrasts possible, management theory will continue to emerge. Common elements will be isolated and important variables brought to light.

We believe that management theory is important to all categories of organizations—business, government, medicine, education, "voluntary" organizations such as the church, and even the home. We thus have drawn our illustrations and cases from a variety of these organizations and incorporated concepts from many disciplines. Our purpose is to identify a framework which may be helpful in integrating independent approaches from these various disciplines to the understanding of human behavior and management theory.

The focus of this book is on behavior *within* organizations and not *between* organizations. Our belief is that an organization is a unique living organism whose basic component is the individual and this individual is our fundamental unit of study. Thus, our concentration is on the interaction of people, motivation, and leadership.

Though this book is an outgrowth of the insights of many earlier writers, we hope it will make some contribution to management theory.

We owe much to colleagues and associates without whose guidance, encouragement, and inspiration this book would not have been written. In particular, we are indebted to Harry Evarts, Ted Hellebrandt, Norman Martin, Don McCarty, Bob Melendes, Warren Ramshaw, and Franklin Williams.

We wish to make special mention of Professor William J. Reddin, The University of New Brunswick, Fredericton, N.B., Canada. His contributions to the field under discussion have been most valuable to us in the course of preparation of this book and we hereby express our appreciation to him.

Finally, we would like to thank our wives for their patience, support, and continued interest in the progress of this book.

PAUL HERSEY

KEN BLANCHARD

Contents

I

MANAGEMENT: A BEHAVIORAL APPROACH

II

MOTIVATION AND BEHAVIOR

III

MOTIVATING ENVIRONMENT

IV

LEADER BEHAVIOR

V

DETERMINING EFFECTIVENESS

VI

MANAGING FOR ORGANIZATIONAL EFFECTIVENESS

1

Management:
A
Behavioral Approach

The transformation of American society since the turn of the century has been breathtaking. We have progressed from a basically agrarian society to a dynamic, industrial society with a higher level of education and standard of living than was ever thought possible. In addition, our scientific and technical advancement staggers the imagination.

This progress has not been without its "seamy side." At a time when we should be rejoicing in a golden age of plenty, we find ourselves wallowing in conflict—conflict between nations, conflict between races, conflict between management and workers, even conflict between neighbors. These problems that we face cannot be solved by scientific and technical skills alone; they will require social skills. Many of our most critical problems are not in the world of *things,* but in the world of *people.* Man's greatest failure has been his inability to secure cooperation and understanding with others. Shortly after the Second World War, Elton Mayo recognized this problem when he reflected that "the consequences for society of the unbalance between the development of technical and of social skill have been disastrous." [1]

SUCCESSFUL VS. UNSUCCESSFUL SCIENCES

In searching for reasons for this unbalance, Mayo suggested that a significant part of the problem might be traced to the difference between what he called "the successful sciences," i.e., chemistry, physics, and physiology and "the unsuccessful sciences," i.e., psychology, sociology, and political science. He labeled the former "successful" because in studying these sciences, both theory and practice are provided. Pure knowledge is limited in value unless it can be applied in real situations. The implication of these profound conclusions is that, in learning about chemistry or physics, a student or practitioner is given direct experience in using his new technical skills in the laboratory. But on the other hand, according to Mayo, the unsuccessful sciences:

> do not seem to equip students with a single social skill that is usable in ordinary human situations . . . no continuous and direct contact with the social facts is contrived for the student. He learns from books, spending endless hours in libraries; he reconsiders ancient formulae, uncontrolled by the steady development of experimental skill, the equivalent of the clinic or indeed of the laboratory.[2]

Change

Early contributions in the behavioral sciences, as Mayo suggests, seemed to provide knowledge without effecting changes in behavior. This book will focus on four levels of change in people: (1) knowledge changes, (2) attitudinal changes, (3) behavior changes, and (4) group or organizational performance changes. The time relationship and relative difficulty involved in making each of these levels of change are illustrated in Figure 1.1.

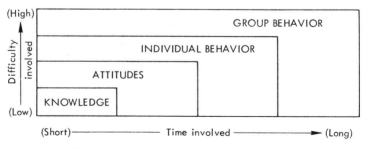

FIGURE 1.1 Time and difficulty involved in making various changes.

Changes in knowledge are the easiest to make, followed by changes in attitudes. Attitude structures differ from knowledge structures in that they are emotionally charged in a positive or negative way. Changes in behavior are significantly more difficult and time consuming than either of the two previous levels. But the implementation of group or organizational performance change is perhaps the most difficult and time consuming. Man's destiny may in fact be dependent upon how well the behavioral sciences are able to resolve conflict through understanding and implementing change.

A Problem of Investment

A major obstacle to the practical application of the behavioral sciences has been the small amount of money allocated by government, business, and other agencies for research in these areas. In the United States, only one of every thirty dollars spent on research and development is channeled to behavioral science areas. The remainder is spent for research in the "hard sciences" to be used in developing "things." However, to be effective, regardless of the type of organization in which they operate, managers need to develop know-how in human skills rather than to increase their knowledge of the technical aspects of their jobs.

MANAGEMENT DEFINED

It is obvious after a review of the literature that there are almost as many definitions of management as there are writers in the field. A common thread which appears in these definitions is the manager's concern for accomplishing organizational goals or objectives.[3] We shall define management as *working with and through individuals and groups to accomplish organizational goals.*

This definition, it should be noted, makes no mention of business or industrial organizations. Management, as defined, applies to organizations whether they are businesses, educational institutions, hospitals, political organizations, or even families. To be successful, these organizations require their management personnel to have interpersonal skills. The achievement of objectives through leadership is management. Thus, everyone is a manager in at least certain portions of his life.

Distinction Between Management and Leadership

Management and leadership are often thought of as one and the same thing. We feel, however, that there is an important distinction between the two concepts.

In essence leadership is a broader concept than management. Management is thought of as a special kind of leadership in which the accomplishment of organizational goals is paramount. The key difference between the two concepts, therefore, lies in the word "organization." While leadership also involves working with and through people to accomplish goals, these goals are not necessarily organizational goals. Many times an individual may attempt to accomplish his own personal goals with little concern for the organization's goals. Hence, one may be successful in accomplishing personal goals, but may be ineffective in terms of accomplishing organizational goals.

MANAGEMENT PROCESS

The managerial functions of *planning, organizing, motivating,* and *controlling* are considered central to a discussion of management by many authors. These functions are relevant, regardless of the type of organization or level of management with which one is concerned. As Harold Koontz and Cyril O'Donnell have said: "Acting in their managerial capacity, presidents, department heads, foremen, supervisors, college deans, bishops, and heads of government agencies all do the same thing." [4] Even a well-run household uses these managerial functions, although in many cases they are used intuitively.

Planning involves setting *goals* and *objectives* for the organization and developing "work maps" showing how these goals and objectives are to be accomplished. Once plans have been made, organizing becomes meaningful. This involves bringing together resources— people, capital, and equipment—in the most effective way to accomplish the goals. Organizing, therefore, involves an integration of resources.

Along with planning and organizing, motivating plays a large part in determining the level of performance of employees which, in turn, influences how effectively the organizational goals will be met.

In his research on motivation, William James of Harvard found that hourly employees could maintain their jobs, that is, not be fired, by working at approximately 20 to 30 per cent of their ability. His study also showed that employees work at close to 80 to 90 per cent of their ability if highly motivated. Both the minimum level at which employees might work and yet keep their jobs and the level at which they could be expected to perform with proper motivation are illustrated in Figure 1.2.

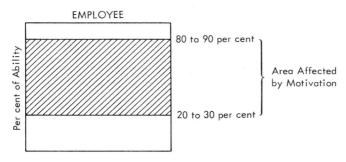

FIGURE 1.2 The potential influence of motivation on performance.

This illustration shows us that if motivation is low, employees' performance will suffer as much as if ability were low. For this reason, motivating is an extremely important function of management.

Another function of management is controlling. This involves feedback of results and follow-up to compare accomplishments with plans and to make appropriate adjustments where outcomes have deviated from expectations.

Even though these management functions are stated separately, and as presented seem to have a specific sequence, one must remember that they are interrelated as illustrated in Figure 1.3. In most cases, these functions occur simultaneously, although, at any one time, one or more may be of primary importance.

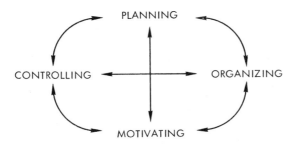

FIGURE 1.3 The process of management.

SKILLS OF A MANAGER

It is generally agreed that there are at least three areas of skill necessary for carrying out the process of management: technical, human, and conceptual skills.

> *Technical skill*—Ability to use knowledge, methods, techniques, and equipment necessary for the performance of specific tasks acquired from experience, education, and training.
>
> *Human skill*—Ability and judgment in working with and through people, including an understanding of motivation, and an application of effective leadership.
>
> *Conceptual skill*—Ability to understand the complexities of the overall organization and where one's own operation fits into the organization. This knowledge permits one to act according to the objectives of the total organization, rather than only on the basis of the goals and needs of one's own immediate group.[5]

The appropriate mix of these skills varies as an individual advances in management from supervisory to top management positions. This is illustrated in Figure 1.4.

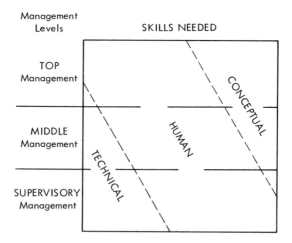

FIGURE 1.4 Management skills necessary at various levels of a business organization.

To be effective less technical skill tends to be needed as one advances from lower to higher levels in the organization, but more and more conceptual skill is necessary. Supervisors at lower levels need considerable technical skill because they are often required to train and develop technicians and other employees in their sections. At the other extreme, executives in a business organization do not need to know how to perform all the specific tasks at the operational level. However, they should be able to see how all these functions are interrelated in accomplishing the goals of the total organization.

While the amount of technical and conceptual skills needed at these different levels of management varies, *the common denominator that appears to be crucial at all levels is human skill.*

Emphasis on Human Skills

This emphasis on human skills was considered important in the past but it is of primary importance today. For example, one of the great entrepreneurs, John D. Rockefeller, stated: "I will pay more for the ability to deal with people than any other ability under the sun." [6] These words of Rockefeller are often echoed. According to a report by the American Management Association, an overwhelming majority of the two hundred managers who participated in a recent survey [7] agreed that the most important single trait of an executive is his ability to get along with people. In this survey, management rated this ability more vital than intelligence, decisiveness, knowledge, or job skills.

Since human skill involves working with and through other people, the main concern of this book will be to help the manager understand why people behave as they do and to increase his effectiveness in predicting future behavior, directing, changing, and controlling behavior. Our intention is to provide a conceptual framework by which the reader can apply conclusions of the behavioral sciences while working with people in his own unique environment.

II

Motivation
and
Behavior

The study of motivation and behavior is a search for answers to perplexing questions about the nature of man. Recognizing the importance of the human element in organizations, we will attempt in this chapter to develop a theoretical framework that may help managers to understand human behavior, not only to determine the "whys" of past behavior, but to some extent to predict, to change, and even to control future behavior.

BEHAVIOR

The basic unit of behavior is an *activity*. In fact, all behavior is a series of activities. As human beings we are always doing something: walking, talking, eating, sleeping, working, and the like. In many instances, we are doing more than one activity at a time, such as talking with someone as we walk or drive to work. At any given moment, we may decide to change from one activity or combination of activities and begin to do something else. This raises some important questions. Why does a person engage in one activity and not another? Why does he change activities? How can we as managers understand, predict, and even control what activity or activities a person may engage in at a given moment in time? To predict behavior managers must know which motives or needs of people evoke a certain action at a particular time.

Behavior is basically goal-oriented. In other words, our behavior is generally motivated by a desire to attain some goal. The specific goal is not always consciously known by the individual. All of us wonder many times, "Why did I do that?" The reason for our action is not always apparent to the conscious mind. The drives that motivate distinctive individual behavioral patterns ("personality") are to a considerable degree subconscious and therefore not easily susceptible to examination and evaluation.

Sigmund Freud was one of the first to recognize the importance of subconscious motivation. He believed that people are not always aware of everything they want, and hence, much of their behavior is affected by subconscious motives or needs. In fact, Freud's research convinced him that an analogy could be drawn between the motivation of most people and the structure of an iceberg. A significant segment of human motivation appears below the surface where it is not always evident to the individual. Therefore, many times only a small portion of motivation is clearly visible or conscious to the individual himself.[8] This may be due to a lack of effort by individuals to gain self-insight. Yet, even with professional help, e.g., psychotherapy, understanding oneself may be a difficult process yielding varying degrees of success.

Motives

People differ not only in their ability to do, but also in their "will to do" or *motivation*. The motivation of a person depends on the strength of his motives. Motives are sometimes defined as needs, wants, drives, desires, or impulses within the individual. Motives are directed toward goals, which may be conscious or subconscious.

Motives are the whys of behavior. They arouse and maintain activity and determine the general direction of the behavior of an individual. In essence, motives or needs are the mainsprings of action. In our discussions we shall use these two terms—motives and needs— interchangeably. In this context, the term "need" should *not* be associated with urgency or any pressing desire for something. It simply means something within an individual which prompts him to action.

Incentives

Goals are *outside* an individual; they are targets toward which motives are directed. These goals are often called *incentives*. Incentives are sometimes referred to as "hoped for" rewards. Managers who are successful in motivating employees are often providing an environment in which proper incentives are available for need satisfaction.

Incentives can be tangible or intangible. Examples of tangible incentives are pay, benefits, and clean surroundings. Praise, sympathy, approval, and feelings of achievement are examples of intangible incentives.

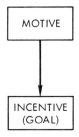

FIGURE 2.1 Motives are directed toward incentives or goals.

Strength of Motives

We have said that motives and needs are the reasons underlying behavior. Every individual has many hundreds of needs. All of these needs compete for his behavior. What then determines which of these motives a person will attempt to satisfy through activity? The need with the *greatest strength* at a particular moment in time leads to activity as illustrated in Figure 2.2, page 12.

Thus, activity is the result of the need with the highest potency. Exceptions may occur when environmental or social pressures deter behavior in this direction. In these cases desired activity is delayed until some more appropriate situation exists. For example, no matter how important a particular meeting is for a manager he may have to delay activity in this direction until the scheduled meeting time.

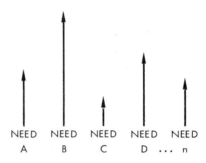

NEED NEED NEED NEED NEED
  A   B   C   D ... n

FIGURE 2.2   The most prepotent need determines behavior (NEED B in this illustration).

Categories of Activity

Behavior can generally be classified into two categories—*goal-directed activity* and *goal activity*. Goal-directed activity, in essence, is behavior directed at reaching a goal. If one's strongest need at a given moment is hunger, various activities such as looking for a place to eat, buying food, or preparing the food would be considered goal-directed activities. On the other hand, goal activity is engaging in the goal itself. In the case of hunger, food is the goal and eating, therefore, is the goal activity.

An important distinction between these two classes of activities is their effect on the strength of the need. In goal-directed activity, the strength of the need tends to increase as one engages in the activity; consider, for example, the hungry person looking for food. The strength of the need tends to build up in goal-directed activity until goal behavior is reached or frustration sets in. Frustration develops when one is continually blocked from reaching a goal. If the frustration becomes intense enough, the strength of the need for that goal may decrease until it no longer is potent enough to affect behavior—a person gives up.

An example of how frustration can affect behavior was dramatically illustrated in an experiment with a fish. A pike was placed in an aquarium with many minnows swimming around him. After the fish became accustomed to the plentiful supply of food, a sheet of glass was placed between the pike and the minnows. When the pike became hungry he tried to reach the minnows but he continually hit his head on the glass. At first the strength of the need for food increased, and the pike tried harder than ever to get the minnows. But finally, his repeated failure of goal attainment resulted in enough frustration that he no longer attempted to eat the minnows. In fact, when the glass partition was finally removed the minnows again swam all around the pike; but no further goal-directed activity took place. Eventually, the pike died of starvation while in the midst of plenty of food.

The strength of the need tends to increase as one engages in goal-directed activity; however, once goal activity begins, the strength of the need tends to decrease as one engages in it. For example, as one eats more and more, the strength of the need for food declines for that particular time. At the point when another need becomes more potent than the present need, behavior changes.

On Thanksgiving Day, for example, as food is being prepared all morning (goal-directed activity), the need for food increases to the point of almost not being able to wait until the meal is on the table. As we begin to eat (goal activity), the strength of this need diminishes to the point where other needs become more important. As we leave the table, our need for food seems to be well satisfied. Our activity changes to that of watching football. This need for passive recreation has now become the most potent and we find ourselves in front of the television set. But gradually this need decreases too. After several games, even though the competition is fierce, the need for passive recreation may also decline to the extent that other needs become more important—perhaps the need for fresh air and a walk, or better still, another piece of pumpkin pie. Several hours before we had sworn not to eat for a week, but now that pie looks mighty good. So once again hunger is the strongest need. Thus, it should be remembered that we never completely satiate a need. We satisfy it only for a period of time.

MOTIVATING SITUATION

The relationship between motives, incentives, and activity can be shown in a simplified fashion as illustrated in Figure 2.3, which follows on page 14.

This schematic illustration shows a *motivating situation* in which the motives of an individual are directed toward goal attainment. The strongest motive produces behavior which is either goal-directed or goal activity. Since all goals are not attainable, individuals do not always reach goal activity, regardless of the strength of the motive. (Thus goal activity is indicated by a dotted line in Figure 2.3.)

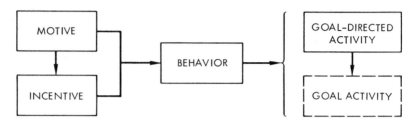

FIGURE 2.3 A motivating situation.

An example of a tangible incentive being used to influence behavior is illustrated in Figure 2.4.

With a broad incentive such as food, it should be recognized that the type of food which satisfies the hunger motive varies from situation to situation. If an individual is starving he may eat anything, while at other times, only a steak will satisfy his hunger motive.

A similar illustration could be given for an intangible incentive. If an individual has a need for recognition—to be viewed as a contributing, productive person—praise is one incentive which will help satisfy this need. In a work situation, if the individual's need for recognition is strong enough, being praised by his manager or supervisor may be an effective incentive in influencing him to continue to do good work.

In analyzing these two examples, it should be remembered that if an individual wants to influence another person's behavior, he must first understand what motives or needs are most important to that person at that time. An incentive to be effective must be appropriate to the need structure of the person involved.

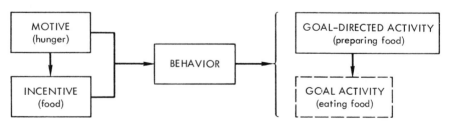

FIGURE 2.4 Use of a tangible incentive in
a motivating situation.

Determinants of Strength of the Motive

We have discussed earlier the strength of needs. Two important factors which affect need strength are expectancy and availability. While these two concepts are interrelated, expectancy tends to affect motives or needs, and availability tends to affect the perception of goals or incentives.

Expectancy is the perceived probability of satisfying a particular need of an individual based on his past experience. Suppose a boy's father was a basketball star and the boy wants to follow in his footsteps. Initially his expectancy may be high and, therefore, the strength of the need is high. If he is cut from the eighth-grade team, it is difficult to determine whether this failure will discourage the boy. Since a single failure is not enough usually to discourage a person (in fact, sometimes results in increased activity), little change in his expectancy is anticipated. But, if he continues to get cut from the team year after year, eventually his expectancy about being a basketball player will decrease. Thus, this motive will no longer be as strong or of such high priority. In fact, after enough unsuccessful experiences, he may completely give up on this goal.

Availability reflects the limitations of the environment. It is determined by how accessible the goals or incentives which can satisfy a given need are in the environment of an individual. For example, if the electricity goes off in a storm, one cannot watch television or read. These goal activities are no longer possible because of the limitations of the environment. You may have a high desire to read but if there is no suitable substitute for the type of illumination required, you will soon be frustrated in your attempts to satisfy this desire and will settle for something else, like sleeping. Consequently, availability is an environmental factor, and thus, is related to incentives.

The expanded diagram of a motivating situation including expectancy and availability is presented in Figure 2.5.

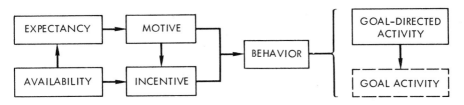

FIGURE 2.5 Expanded diagram of a motivating situation.

PERSONALITY DEVELOPMENT

As an individual matures he develops habit patterns or conditioned responses to various stimuli. The sum of these habit patterns
determines his *personality*.

habit a, *habit* b, *habit* c . . . *habit* n = *personality*

As an individual begins to behave in a similar fashion under similar conditions, this behavior is what others learn to recognize as that
person, as his personality. They expect and even can predict certain
kinds of behavior from him.

Changing Personality

Many psychologists contend that basic personality structures are
developed quite early in life. In fact, some claim that few personality
changes can be made after age seven or eight. Using a model similar
to the one appearing in Figure 2.5, we can begin to understand why
it tends to become more difficult to make changes in personality as
people grow older.

Note that in this model we are using *sum of past experience* in
place of the term *expectancy* used in the earlier model. These can
be used interchangeably.

When a person behaves in a motivating situation, that behavior
becomes a *new* input to his inventory of past experience, as the feedback loop in Figure 2.6 indicates. The earlier in life that this input
occurs, the greater its potential effect on future behavior. The reason
is, at that time, this behavior represents a larger portion of the total
past experience of a young person than the same behavior input would
later in life. In addition, the longer behavior is reinforced, the more
patterned it becomes and more difficult it is to change. That is why it
is easier to make personality changes early in life. The older a person
gets the more time and new experiences are necessary to effect a
change in behavior.

While it is possible to change behavior in older people, it will
be difficult to accomplish except over a long period of time under

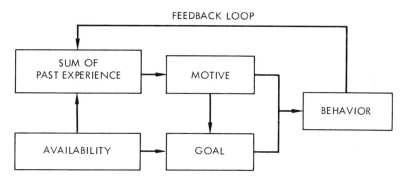

FIGURE 2.6 Feedback model.

conducive conditions. It almost becomes a matter of economics. How much can be invested in implementing such a change? An illustration might be helpful. Putting one new input, a drop of red coloring, into a half pint bottle of clear liquid may be enough to change drastically the appearance of the total contents. Adding the same input, a drop of red coloring, to a gallon jug may make little, if any, noticeable change in its appearance to others. Although this example does not concern behavior, it does illustrate the relationship between the amount of past experience and the effect of any one new experience.

HIERARCHY OF NEEDS

We have argued that the behavior of an individual at a particular moment is usually determined by his strongest need. It would seem significant, therefore, for managers to have some understanding about the needs which are commonly most important to people.

An interesting framework which helps explain the strength of certain needs was developed by Abraham Maslow.[9] According to Maslow, there seems to be a hierarchy into which human needs arrange themselves as illustrated in Figure 2.7, page 18.

The *physiological* needs are shown at the top of the hierarchy because they tend to have the highest strength until they are somewhat satisfied. These are the basic human needs to sustain life itself—food, clothing, shelter. Until these basic needs are satisfied to the degree needed for the sufficient operation of the body, the majority of a person's activity will probably be at this level, and the other levels will provide him with little motivation.

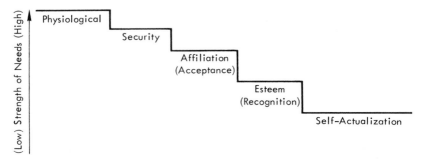

FIGURE 2.7 Maslow's hierarchy of needs.

But what happens to a man's motivation when these basic needs begin to be fulfilled? Rather than physiological needs, other levels of needs become important and these motivate and dominate the behavior of the individual. And, when these needs are somewhat satiated, other needs emerge, and so on down the hierarchy.

Once physiological needs become gratified the security or safety needs become predominant as illustrated in Figure 2.8. These needs are essentially the need to be free of the fear of physical danger and deprivation of the basic physiological needs. In other words, this is a need for self-preservation. In addition to the here and now, there is a concern for the future. Will an individual be able to maintain his property and/or job so he can provide food and shelter tomorrow and the next day? If a man's safety or security is in danger, other things seem unimportant.

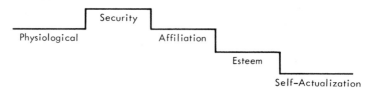

FIGURE 2.8 Security need when dominant in the need structure.

Once physiological and security needs are fairly well satisfied, affiliation or acceptance will emerge as dominant in the need structure as illustrated in Figure 2.9. Since man is a social being, he has a need

FIGURE 2.9 Affiliation need when dominant in the need structure.

to belong, and to be accepted by various groups. When affiliation needs become dominant a person will strive for meaningful relations with others.

After an individual begins to satisfy his need to belong, he generally wants to be more than just a member of his group. He then feels the need for *esteem*—both self-esteem and recognition from others. Most people have a need for a high evaluation of themselves that is firmly based in reality—recognition and respect from others. Satisfaction of these esteem needs produces feelings of self-confidence, prestige, power, and control. One begins to feel that he is useful and has some effect on his environment. There are other occasions, though, when persons are unable to satisfy their need for esteem through constructive behavior. When this need is dominant an individual may resort to disruptive or immature behavior to satisfy his desire for attention —a child may throw a temper tantrum, an employee may engage in work restriction or arguments with his co-workers or boss. Thus, recognition is not always obtained through mature or adaptive behavior. It is sometimes garnered by disruptive and irresponsible actions. In fact, some of the social problems we have today may have their roots in the frustration of esteem needs.

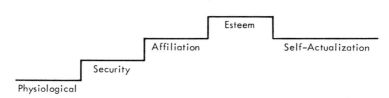

FIGURE 2.10 Esteem need when dominant in the need structure.

Once esteem needs begin to be adequately satisfied, the self-actualization needs become more prepotent, as shown in Figure 2.11. Self-actualization is the need to maximize one's potential, whatever it may be: A musician must play music, a poet must write, a general must win battles, a professor must teach. As Maslow expressed it, "What a man *can* be, he *must* be." Thus self-actualization is the desire to become what one is capable of becoming. Individuals satisfy this need in different ways. In one person it may be expressed in the desire to be an ideal mother, in another it may be expressed in managing an organization, in another it may be expressed athletically, in still another by playing the piano.

In combat, a soldier might put his life on the line and rush a machine-gun nest in an attempt to destroy it, knowing full well that his chances for survival are low. He is not doing it for affiliation or recognition, but rather for what he thinks is important. In this case, you might consider the soldier to have self-actualized—to be maximizing the potential of what is important to him.

The way self-actualization is expressed can change over the life cycle. For example, the self-actualized athlete may eventually look for other areas in which to maximize his potential as his physical attributes change over time or as his horizons broaden. In addition, the hierarchy does not necessarily follow the pattern described by Maslow. It was not his intent to say that this hierarchy applies universally. Maslow felt this was a *typical* pattern that operates most of the time. He realizes, however, that there were numerous exceptions to this general tendency. For example, the late Indian leader, Mahatma Gandhi, frequently sacrificed his physiological and safety needs for the satisfaction of other needs when India was striving for independence from Great Britain. In his historical fasts, Gandhi went weeks without nourishment to protest governmental injustices. He was operating at the self-actualization level while some of his other needs were unsatisfied.

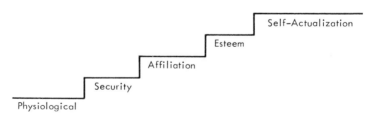

FIGURE 2.11 Self-actualization when dominant in the need structure.

In discussing the preponderance of one need over another, we have been careful to speak in such terms as "if one level of needs has been somewhat gratified, then other needs emerge as dominant." This was done because we did not want to give the impression that one level of needs has to be completely satisfied before the next level emerges as the most important. In reality, most people in our society tend to be partially satisfied at each level and partially unsatisfied, with greater satisfaction tending to occur at the physiological and safety levels than at the affiliation, esteem, and self-actualization levels. For example, a person could be described as 85 per cent satisfied in his physiological needs, 70 per cent satisfied in his safety needs, 50 per cent in his acceptance needs, 40 per cent in his recognition needs, and 10 per cent in his self-actualization needs.[10] These percentages are used only for illustrative reasons. In reality they vary tremendously from one individual to another.

MOTIVATIONAL RESEARCH

Having discussed Maslow's hierarchy of needs, we can now examine what researchers say about some of our motives and the incentives which tend to satisfy them.

Physiological Needs

The satisfaction of physiological needs (shelter, food, clothing) are usually associated in our society with *money*. It is obvious that most people are not interested in dollars as such, but only as a tool to be used to satisfy other motives. Thus, it is what money can buy, not money itself, that satisfies one's physiological needs. To suggest that money as a tool is useful *only* to satisfy physiological needs would be short-sighted, because money can play a role in the satisfaction of needs at every level. Extensive studies of the impact of money have found that money is so complicated an incentive that it is entangled with all kinds of needs besides physiological ones, and its importance is difficult to ascertain. Consequently, we will discuss the money motive in a separate section later in the chapter. It is clear, however, that the ability of a given amount of money to satisfy *seems* to diminish as one moves from physiological and safety needs to other needs on the hierarchy. In many cases, money can buy the satisfaction of physiological and safety needs and even belongingness, if, for example, it provides entry into a desired group such as a country club. But as one becomes concerned about esteem, recognition, and eventually self-actualization, money becomes a less appropriate tool to satisfy these needs and, therefore, less effective. The more an individual becomes involved with esteem and self-actualization needs, the more he will have to earn his satisfaction directly and thus, the less important money will be in their attainment.

Security

We mentioned earlier that motives are not always apparent to the individual. Although some motives appear above the surface, many are largely subconscious and are not obvious or easy to identify. According to Saul W. Gellerman, security needs appear in both forms.[11]

The conscious security needs are quite evident and very common among most people. We all have a desire to remain free from the hazards of life—accidents, wars, diseases, and economic instability. Therefore, individuals and organizations are interested in providing some assurance that these catastrophes will be avoided if possible. Gellerman suggests that many organizations tend to overemphasize the security motive by providing elaborate programs of fringe benefits such as health, accident, and life insurance, and retirement plans. While such emphasis on security may make people more docile and predictable, it does not mean they will be more productive. In fact, if creativity or initiative is necessary in their jobs, an overemphasis on security can thwart desired behavior.

While concern for security can affect major decisions such as remaining in or leaving an organization, Gellerman indicates it is not likely to be an individual's dominant motive. Conscious security needs usually play a background role, often inhibiting or restraining impulses, rather than initiating outward behavior. For example, if a particular course of action, such as disregarding a rule or expressing an unpopular position, might endanger one's job, then security considerations motivate a person *not* to take this course of action. Organizations can influence these security needs either positively—through pension plans, insurance programs, and the like—or negatively by arousing fears of being fired or laid off, demoted, or passed over. In both cases, the effect can be to make behavior too cautious and conservative.

Peter F. Drucker suggests that one's attitude toward security is important to consider in choosing a job.[12] He raises some interesting questions: Do you belong in a job calling primarily for faithfulness in the performance of routine work and promising security? Do you find real satisfaction in the precision, order, and system of a clearly laid-out job? Do you prefer the security not only of knowing what your work is today and what it is going to be tomorrow, but also security in your job, in your relationship to the people above, below, and next to you? Or do you belong in a job that offers a challenge to imagination and ingenuity—with the attendant penalty for failure? Are you one of those people who tend to grow impatient with anything that looks like a "routine" job? The answers to these questions are not always easy even though we all understand ourselves to some degree. But the answers are involved with how important the security motive is for that particular individual.

To reiterate, security needs can be conscious or subconscious. A strong subconscious orientation toward security is often developed early in childhood. Gellerman discusses several ways in which it can be implanted. A common way is through identification with security-minded parents who are willing to accept whatever fate comes along. This often occurs in depressed economic areas where the prospects for improvement are poor.[13]

The world seems uncertain and uncontrollable to people raised in a security-minded home. As a result, such people may not feel they are competent enough to be able to influence their environment.

The security-minded person we have been describing is often very likeable. He is not competitive and, therefore, does not put people on the defense. Others tend to expect little of him, and thus are seldom critical of his work. This, combined with the fact that he is pleasant to have around, often enables him to obtain a secure, nonthreatening position in an organization.

Subconscious security motives may also develop in a child through interaction with over-protective parents. Such parents are constantly trying to shield their children from heartache, disappointment, or failure. The supportive attitude of these parents in many instances permits their children to have their own way. Conflict is avoided at all costs. As a result, the child is given a distorted picture of reality, and gains little insight into what he can expect of other people and what they will expect of him. In some cases, he becomes unrealistic in his optimism about life. Even in the face of disaster, when he should be threatened, he seems to believe that all is well until too late.

When this type of security-minded person leaves home after high school to seek his way in the world, he quickly wakes up to reality. Often he finds himself unequipped to handle the hardships of life because he has *not* been permitted the opportunity to develop the capacity to handle frustration, tension, and anxiety. As a result, even a minor set back may throw him for a loss. Drucker suggests that getting fired from their first job might be the best thing that could happen to such young people. He feels that getting fired from the first job is the least painful and least damaging way to learn how to take a set back and that this is a lesson well worth learning. If a person learns how to recover from seeming disaster when he is young, he will be better equipped to handle worse fate as he gets older.

To many people, the security motive carries with it a negative connotation. A strong security need is frowned upon, for some reason, as if it were less respectable than other motives. This seems unjust, especially since nearly everyone has some conscious and subconscious security motives. Life is never so simple or clear-cut that one does not maintain some concern for security. In addition, many segments of our society often cater to these needs to the exclusion of such important needs as affiliation and self-actualization. We have already mentioned how industry concentrates on security needs by providing elaborate fringe benefits. Unions have a similar effect with their emphasis on seniority, and the government does much the same thing with welfare and "great society" programs.

Affiliation

After the physiological and safety needs have become somewhat satisfied, the affiliation needs may become predominant. Since man is a social animal, most people like to interact and be with others in situations where they feel they belong and are accepted. While this is a common need, it tends to be stronger for some people than others and stronger in certain situations. In other words, even such a commonplace social need as belongingness is, upon examination, quite complex.

In working toward a better understanding of our need to belong, Stanley Schachter of the University of Minnesota has made a significant contribution.[14] His efforts, in particular, have been directed toward studying the desire to socialize as an end in itself—that is when people interact simply because they enjoy it. In some of these situations no apparent reward such as money or protection was gained from this affiliation.

Schachter found that it was not always simply good fellowship that motivated affiliation. In many instances, people seek affiliation because they desire to have their beliefs confirmed. People who have similar beliefs tend to seek each other out, especially if a strongly held belief had been shattered. In this case, they tend to assemble and try to reach some common understanding about what happened and what they should believe (even if it is the same as before). In this instance, the need for affiliation was prompted by a desire to make one's life *seem* a little more under control. When alone, the world seems "out of whack," but if one can find an environment where others hold the same beliefs, it somehow makes order out of chaos. This attitude hints at some of the problems inherent in any change.

In pursuing this question further, it was found that when people are excited, confused, or unhappy, they don't just seek out anyone, they tend to want to be with others "in the same boat." Misery doesn't just love company, it loves other miserable people. These conclusions suggest that the strong informal work groups that Elton Mayo found developing in the factory system might have been a reaction to the boredom, insignificance, and lack of competence which the workers felt.[15] As a result, workers congregated because of mutual feelings of being beaten by the system.

In observing "loners" and "rate-busters" in similar factory situations, it became apparent that there is not some universal need for affiliation as an end in itself. It was found, however, that these exceptions to the affiliation tendency were special types of people. They tended not to join informal work groups because they felt either suspicious or contemptuous of them, or secure and competent enough to fend for themselves.

Management is often suspicious of informal groups that develop at work because of the potential power these groups have to lower productivity. Schachter found that such work restricting groups were sometimes formed as a reaction to the insignificance and impotence which workers tend to feel when they have no control over their working environment. Such environments develop where the work is routine, tedious, and oversimplified. This situation is made worse when, at the same time, the workers are closely supervised and controlled, but have no clear channels of communication with management.

In this type of environment, workers who cannot tolerate this lack of control over their environment depend on the informal group for support of unfulfilled needs such as affiliation or achievement. Work restriction follows not from an inherent dislike for management, but as a means to preserve the identification of individuals within the group and the group itself. Rate-busters are not tolerated because they weaken the group and its power with management, and to weaken the group destroys the only dignity, security, and significance the worker feels he has.

Lowering productivity is not always the result of informal work groups. In fact, informal groups can be a tremendous asset to management if their internal organization is understood and fully utilized. The productivity of a work group seems to depend on how the group members see their own goals in relation to the goals of the organization. For example, if they perceive their own goals as being in conflict with the goals of the organization, then productivity will tend to be low. However, if these workers see their own goals as being the same as the goals of the organization or as being satisfied as a direct result of accomplishing organizational goals, then productivity will tend to be high. Work restriction is therefore not a necessary aspect of informal work groups.

Esteem

The need for esteem or recognition appears in a number of forms. In this section we shall discuss two motives related to esteem—prestige and power.

Prestige

The prestige motive is becoming more evident in our society today, especially as we move more toward a middle-class society. People with a concern for prestige want to "keep up with the Joneses"; in fact, given the choice, they'd like to stay ahead of the Joneses. Vance Packard [16] and David Riesman [17] probably had the greatest impact in exposing prestige motivation. Packard wrote about the status-seekers and their motives, while Riesman unveiled "other-directed" individuals who were part of "the lonely crowd."

What exactly is prestige? Gellerman describes it as "A sort of unwritten definition of the kinds of conduct that other people are expected to show in one's presence: what degree of respect or disrespect, formality or informality, reserve or frankness." [18] Prestige seems to have an effect on how comfortably or conveniently one can expect to get along in life.

Prestige is something intangible bestowed upon an individual by society. In fact, at birth a child inherits the status of his parents. In some cases, this is enough to carry him through life on "a prestige-covered wave." For example, a Rockefeller or a Ford inherits instant prestige with his family background.

People seek prestige throughout their lives in various ways. Many tend to seek only the material symbols of status, while others strive for personal achievement or self-actualization which might command prestige in itself. Regardless of the way it is expressed, there seems to be a widespread need for people to have their importance clarified and, in fact, set at a level which each feels he deserves. As discussed earlier, people normally want to have a high evaluation of themselves which is firmly based in reality as manifested by the recognition and respect accorded them by others.

The need for prestige is more or less self-limiting. People tend to seek prestige only to a preconceived level. When they feel they have gained this level, the strength of this need tends to decline and prestige becomes a matter of maintenance rather than of further advancement. Some people can become satisfied with their level of importance in their company and community. In their own evaluation, "they have arrived." Only the exceptional seek national or international recognition. Prestige motivation therefore often appears in young people who tend not to be satisfied yet with their status in life. Older people tend to have reached a level of prestige which satisfies them or they become resigned to the fact that they can do little to improve their status.[19]

Power

There tends to be two kinds of power—position and personal. An individual who is able to influence the behavior of another because of his position in the organization has *position* power, while an individual who derives his influence from his personality and behavior has *personal* power. Some people are endowed with both types of power. Still others seem to have no power at all.

Alfred Adler, a one-time colleague of Freud, became very interested in this power motive.[20] By power Adler essentially meant the ability to manipulate or control the activities of others to suit one's own purposes. He found that this ability starts at an early age when a baby realizes that if he cries he influences his parents' behavior. The child's position as a baby gives him considerable power over his parents.

According to Adler, this manipulative ability is inherently pleasurable. A child, for example, often has a hard time adjusting to the continuing reduction in his position power. In fact, he might spend a significant amount of time as an adult trying to recapture the power he had as a child. However, Adler did not feel that a child seeks power for its own sake as often as he does out of necessity. Power, for a child, is often a life-and-death matter because he is helpless and needs to count on his parents' availability. Parents are a child's life line. Thus, power acquires an importance in children that they somehow never lose, even though they later are able to fend for themselves.

After childhood, the power motive again becomes very potent in individuals who feel somehow inadequate in winning the respect and recognition of others. These people go out of their way to seek attention to overcome this weakness which is often felt but not recognized. In this connection, Adler introduced two interesting and now well-known concepts in his discussion—*inferiority complex* and *compensation*.

A person with an inferiority complex has underlying fears of inadequacy which may or may not have some basis in reality. In some cases, individuals compensate for this inferiority complex by exerting extreme efforts to achieve goals or objectives which (they feel) inadequacy would deny. In many cases extreme effort seems to be an overcompensation for something not clearly perceived although felt. Once accurately perceived, the frame of reference can be realigned with reality and result in more realistic behavior.

Adler found another interesting thing. If a child does not encounter too much tension as he matures, his need for power gradually transforms itself into a desire to perfect his social relationships. He wants to be able to interact with others without fear or suspicion in an open and trusting atmosphere. Thus, an individual often moves from the *task* aspect of power, wanting to structure and manipulate his environment and the people in it, to a concern for *relationships,* developing trust and respect for others. This transformation is often delayed with individuals who have had tension-filled childhoods and have not learned to trust. In these cases, the power motive would not only persist but might even become stronger. Thus Adler, like Freud, felt that the personality of an individual is developed early in life and is often a result of the kind of experiences the child had with adults in his world.

Self-Actualization

Of all the needs discussed by Maslow, the one which social and behavioral scientists know least about is self-actualization. Perhaps this is a result of the fact that people satisfy this need in different ways. Thus, self-actualization is a difficult need to pin down and identify.

While little research has been done on the concept of self-actualization, extensive research has been done on two motives which the authors feel are related to it—*competence* and *achievement*.

Competence

According to Robert W. White, one of the mainsprings of action in a human being is a desire for competence.[21] Competence implies control over environmental factors—both physical and social. People with this motive do not wish to wait passively for things to happen; they want to be able to manipulate their environment and make things happen.

The competence motive can be identified in young children as they move from the early stage of wanting to touch and handle everything in reach to the later stage of wanting, not only to touch, but to take things apart and put them back together again. He begins to learn his way around his world. He becomes aware of what he can do and cannot do. This is not in terms of what he is allowed to do, but in terms of what he is able to do. During these early years a child develops a feeling of competence.

This feeling of competence is closely related to the concept of expectancy discussed earlier. Whether a child's sense of competence is strong or weak depends on his successes and failures in the past. If his successes overshadow his failures, then his feeling of competence will tend to be high. He will have a positive outlook toward life, seeing almost every new situation as an interesting challenge which he can overcome. If, however, his failures carry the day, his outlook will be more negative and expectancy for satisfying various needs may become low. Since expectancy tends to influence motives, people with low feelings of competence will not often be motivated to seek new challenges or take risks. These people would rather let their environment control them than attempt to change it.

The sense of competence, while established early in life, is not necessarily permanent. White found that unexpected good or bad fortune may influence one's feelings of competence in a positive or negative way. Thus, the competence motive tends to be cumulative. For example, a person can get off to a bad start and then develop a strong sense of competence because of new successes. There is, however, a point in time when a sense of competence seems to stabilize itself. When this occurs, the sense of competence almost becomes a self-fulfilling prophecy, influencing whether a given experience will be a success or a failure. After a person reaches a certain age, he seldom achieves more than he thinks he can, because he does not attempt things he thinks he cannot achieve.

According to White, the competence motive reveals itself in adults as a desire for job mastery and professional growth. An individual's job is one arena where he can match his ability and skills against his environment in a contest which is challenging but not overwhelming. In jobs where such a contest is possible, the competence motive in an individual can be expressed freely and significant personal rewards can be gained. But in routine, closely supervised jobs, this contest is often impossible. Such situations make the worker dependent on the system and therefore completely frustrate people with high competence needs.

Achievement

Over the years behavioral scientists have observed that some people have an intense need to achieve; others, perhaps the majority, do not seem to be as concerned about achievement. This phenomenon fascinated David C. McClelland. For over twenty years he and his associates at Harvard University have been studying this urge to achieve.[22]

McClelland's research has led him to believe that the need for achievement is a distinct human motive that can be distinguished from other needs. More important, the achievement motive can be isolated and assessed in any group.

What are some of the characteristics of people with a high need for achievement? McClelland illustrates some of these characteristics in describing a laboratory experiment. Participants were asked to throw rings over a peg from any distance they chose. Most men tended to throw randomly, now close, now far away; but individuals with a high need for achievement seemed to carefully measure where they were most likely to get a sense of mastery—not too close to make the task ridiculously easy or too far away to make it impossible. They set moderately difficult but potentially achievable goals. In biology, this is known as the "overload principle." In weightlifting, for example, strength cannot be increased by tasks which can be performed easily or which cannot be performed without injury to the organism. Strength can be increased by lifting weights which are difficult but realistic enough to "stretch" the muscles.

Do people with a high need for achievement behave like this all the time? No. Only if they can influence the outcome. Achievement-motivated people are not gamblers. They prefer to work on a problem rather than leave the outcome to chance.

In terms of a manager, setting moderately difficult but potentially achievable goals may be translated into an attitude toward risks. Many people tend to be extreme in their attitude toward risks, either favoring wild speculative gambling or minimizing their exposure to losses. The gambler seems to choose the big risk because the outcome is beyond his power and, therefore, he can easily rationalize away his personal responsibility if he loses. The conservative individual chooses tiny risks where the gain is small but secure, perhaps because there is little danger of anything going wrong for which he might be blamed. The achievement-motivated person takes the middle-ground, preferring a moderate degree of risk because he feels his efforts and abilities will probably influence the outcome. In business, this aggressive realism is the mark of the successful entrepreneur.

Another characteristic of the achievement-motivated person is that he seems to be more concerned with personal achievement than with the rewards of success. While he does not reject rewards, they are not as essential for him as the accomplishment itself. He gets a bigger "kick" out of winning or solving a difficult problem than he gets from any money or praise he receives. Money, to the achievement-motivated person, is valuable to him primarily as a measurement of his performance. It provides him with a means of assessing his progress and comparing his achievements with those of other people. He normally does not seek money for status or economic security.

A desire by people with a high need for achievement to seek situations in which they get concrete feedback on how well they are doing is closely related to this concern for personal accomplishment. Consequently, achievement-motivated people are often found in sales jobs or as owners and managers of their own business. In addition to concrete feedback, the nature of the feedback is important to achievement-motivated people. They respond favorably to information about their work. They are not interested in comments about their personal characteristics, such as how cooperative or helpful they are. Affiliation-motivated people might want "social" or attitudinal feedback. Achievement-motivated people want task-relevant feedback. They want to know the score.

Why do achievement-motivated people behave as they do? McClelland claims because they habitually spend time thinking about doing things better. He has found, in fact, that wherever people start to think in achievement terms, things start to happen. Examples can be cited. College students with a high need for achievement will generally get better grades than equally bright students with weaker achievement needs. Achievement-motivated men tend to get more raises and are promoted faster because they are constantly trying to think of better ways of doing things. Companies with many such men grow faster and are more profitable. McClelland has even extended his analysis to countries where he related the presence of a large percentage of achievement-motivated individuals to the national economic growth.

McClelland has found that achievement-motivated people are more likely to be found in certain groups or classes of society than in others. He found that middle-class families (the merchants, managers, professionals, and salaried specialists of all kinds) seem to breed these kinds of children more than the other socio-economic classes. Perhaps this is why our country continues to grow economically and socially. After all, we are gradually becoming a nation of middle-class people.

McClelland discovered that middle-class parents hold different expectations for their children than do other parents. More importantly, they expect their children to start showing some independence between the ages of six and eight, making choices and doing things without help such as knowing the way around the neighborhood and taking care of themselves around the house. Other parents tend to either expect this too early, before the child is ready, or smother the development of the personality of the child. One extreme seemed to foster a passive, defeated attitude as the child felt unwanted at home and incompetent away from home. He was just not ready for that kind of independence so early. The other extreme, yielded either an overprotected or overdisciplined child. The child became very dependent on his parents and found it difficult to break away and make his own decisions.

Given all we know about the need for achievement, can this motive be taught and developed in people? McClelland is convinced that this can be done. In fact, he has already developed training programs for businessmen that are designed to increase their achievement motivation. He is also in the process of developing similar programs for other segments of the population. These programs could have tremendous implications for training and developing human resources.

While achievement-motivated people can be the backbone of most organizations, what can we say about their potential as managers? As we know, a person with a high need for achievement gets ahead because as an individual he is a producer. He gets things done. However, when he is promoted to a position where his success not only depends on his own work but the activities of others, he may be less effective. Since he is highly task-oriented and works to his capacity, he tends to expect others to do the same. As a result, he sometimes lacks the human skills and patience necessary for being an effective manager of people who are competent but have a higher need for affiliation than he does. In this situation his high task-low relationships behavior frustrates and prohibits these people from maximizing their own potentials. Thus, while achievement-motivated people are needed in organizations, they do not always make the best managers.

Money Motive

As stated earlier, money is a very complicated motive which is entangled in such a way with all kinds of needs besides physiological needs that its importance is often difficult to ascertain. For example, in some cases, money can provide an individual with certain material things such as a fancy sports car from which he can gain a feeling of affiliation (joins a sports car club), recognition (status symbol), and even self-actualization (becomes an outstanding sports car driver). Consequently, we delayed our discussion of the money motive until other basic concepts were clarified.

From extensive research on incentive pay schemes, William F. White has found that money, the "old reliable" motivational tool, is not as "all mighty" as it is supposed to be, particularly for production workers.[23] For each of these workers, another key factor, as Mayo discovered, is his work group. Using the ratio of high producing "rate-busters" to low-producing "restrictors" as an index, White estimates that only about ten per cent of the production workers in the United States will ignore group pressure and produce as much as possible in response to an incentive plan. It seems that while the worker *is* interested in advancing his own financial position, there are many other considerations, such as the opinions of his fellow workers, his comfort and enjoyment on the job, and his long range security, which prevent him from making a direct, automatic, positive response to an incentive plan.

According to Gellerman, the most subtle and most important characteristic of money is its power as a symbol.[24] Its most obvious symbolic power is its market value. It is what money can buy, not money itself, that gives it value. But, money's symbolic power is not limited to its market value. Since money has no intrinsic meaning of its own, it can symbolize almost any need an individual wants it to represent. In other words, money can mean whatever people want it to mean.

WHAT DO WORKERS WANT FROM THEIR JOBS?

In talking about motives it is important to remember that people have many needs, all of which are continually competing for their behavior. No one person has exactly the same mixture or strength of these needs. There are some people who are driven mainly by money; others who are concerned primarily with security, and so on. While we must recognize individual differences, this does not mean that, as managers, we cannot make some predictions about which motives seem to be currently more prominent among our employees than others. According to Maslow, these are prepotent motives—those that are still *not* satisfied. (Satisfied needs decrease in strength and normally do not motivate individuals to seek goals or incentives to satisfy them.) An important question for managers to answer is: "What do workers really want from their jobs?"

Some interesting research has been conducted among employees in American industry in an attempt to answer this question. In one such study, supervisors were asked to try to put themselves in a *worker's* shoes by ranking in order of importance a series of items which describe things workers may want from their jobs. It was emphasized that in ranking the items the supervisors should *not* think in terms of what they want but what they think a worker wants. In addition to the supervisors, the workers themselves were asked to rank these same items in terms of what *they* wanted most from their jobs. The results are given in Table 2.1. (1 = highest and 10 = lowest in importance.)

As is evident from the results, supervisors generally ranked wages, job security, promotion and working conditions as the things workers want most from their jobs. On the other hand, workers felt that what they wanted most was full appreciation of work done, feeling "in" on things, and sympathetic understanding of personal problems—all incentives which seem to be related to affiliation and recognition motives. It is interesting to note that these things which workers indicated they wanted most from their jobs were rated by their foremen as least important. In some cases, there seems to be very little sensitivity by supervisors as to what things are really most important to workers. Supervisors seem to think that incentives directed to satisfy physiological and safety motives tend to be most important to their workers.

	Supervisors	*Workers*
Good working conditions	4	9
Feeling "in" on things	10	2
Tactful disciplining	7	10
Full appreciation for work done	8	1
Management loyalty to workers	6	8
Good wages	1	5
Promotion and growth with company	3	7
Sympathetic understanding of personal problems .	9	3
Job security	2	4
Interesting work	5	6

TABLE 2.1   What do workers want from their jobs?

Since supervisors perceive workers as having these motives, supervisors act as if they were true. Therefore, supervisors use the "old reliable" incentives—money, fringe benefits and security to motivate workers.

One might generalize at this point that individuals act on the basis of their perceptions and *not* on reality. By bringing his perception closer and closer to reality—what his men really want—a manager can often increase his effectiveness in working with employees. A manager has to know his people to understand what motivates them; he cannot just make assumptions. Even if a manager asked an employee how he felt about something, this does not necessarily result in relevant feedback. The quality of communications a manager receives from his employees is often based upon the rapport which has been established between his men and himself over a long period of time.

It is becoming clearer that many managers do not realize or understand that what people want from their jobs today is different from what they wanted a few decades ago. Today in the United States, few people, with the exception of those in some of the urban ghettos and poverty belts, have to worry about where their next meal will come from or whether they will be protected from the elements or physical dangers. The satisfaction of physiological and safety needs has been the result of the tremendous rise in our standard of living, dramatic increases in pay and fringe benefits at all levels of work, and extensive aid from governmental programs—welfare, social security, medicare, and unemployment insurance. In addition, the union movement and labor laws have made significant strides in assuring safe working conditions and job security.

Our society almost has a built-in guarantee of physiological and safety needs for large segments of the population. Since many physiological and safety needs have been provided for, it is understandable why people today have become more concerned with social, recognition, and self-actualization motives. Managers must become aware of this fact. Because of employees' changing need priorities, today's organizations should provide the kind of environment that will motivate and satisfy more than just physiological and security needs. In Chapter 3 we will describe some of the research which may be helpful to a manager in building a motivating environment that will increase organizational effectiveness.

III

Motivating Environment

In 1924 efficiency experts at the Hawthorne, Illinois, plant of the Western Electric Company designed a research program to study the effects of illumination on productivity. At first, nothing about this program seemed exceptional enough to arouse any unusual interest. After all, efficiency experts had long been trying to find the ideal mix of physical conditions, working hours, and working methods which stimulate workers to produce at maximum capacity. Yet, by the time these studies were completed (over a decade later), there was little doubt that the work at Hawthorne would stand the test of time as one of the most exciting and important research projects ever done in an industrial setting. For it was at Western Electric's Hawthorne plant that the Human Relations Movement began to gather momentum, and one of its early advocates, Elton Mayo of the Harvard Graduate School of Business Administration, gained recognition.[25]

HAWTHORNE STUDIES
Elton Mayo

In the initial study at Hawthorne, efficiency experts assumed that increases in illumination would result in higher output. Two groups of employees were selected: an *experimental* or *test group* which worked under varying degrees of light, and a *control group* which worked under normal illumination conditions in the plant. As lighting power was increased, the output of the test group went up as anticipated. Unexpectedly, however, the output of the control group went up also—without any increase in light.

Determined to explain these and other surprising test results, the efficiency experts decided to expand their research at Hawthorne. They felt, that in addition to technical and physical changes, some of the behavioral considerations should be explored, so Mayo and his associates were called in to help.

Mayo and his team started their experiments with a group of girls who assembled telephone relays, and, like the efficiency experts, the Harvard men uncovered astonishing results. For over a year-and-a-half during this experiment, Mayo's researchers improved the working conditions of the girls by implementing such innovations as scheduled rest periods, company lunches, and shorter work weeks. Baffled by the results, the researchers suddenly decided to take everything away from the girls, returning the working conditions to the exact way they had been at the beginning of the experiment. This radical change was expected to have a tremendous negative psychological impact on the girls, and reduce their output. Instead, their output jumped to a new *all-time high*. Why?

The answers to his question were *not* found in the production aspects of the experiment (i.e. changes in plant and physical working conditions), but in the *human* aspects. As a result of the attention lavished upon them by experimenters, the girls were made to feel they were an important part of the company. They no longer viewed themselves as isolated individuals, working together only in the sense that they were physically close to each other. Instead they had become participating members of a congenial, cohesive work group. The relationships which developed elicited feelings of affiliation, competence, and achievement. These needs, which had long gone unsatisfied at work, were now being fulfilled. The girls worked harder and more effectively than they had worked previously.

Realizing that they had uncovered an interesting phenomenon, the Harvard team extended their research by interviewing over twenty thousand employees from every department in the company. Interviews were designed to help researchers find out what the workers thought about their jobs, their working conditions, their supervisors, their company, and anything that bothered them, and how these feelings might be related to their productivity. After several interview sessions, Mayo's group found that a structured question-and-answer type interview was useless for eliciting the information they wanted. Instead, the workers wanted to talk freely about what *they* thought was important. So the predetermined questions were discarded, and the interviewer allowed the worker to ramble as he chose.

The interviews proved valuable in a number of ways. First of all, they were therapeutic; the workers got an opportunity to get a lot off their chests. Many felt this was the best thing the company had ever done. The result was a wholesale change in attitude. Since many of their suggestions were being implemented, the workers began to feel that management viewed them as important, both as individuals and as a group; they were now participating in the operation and future of the company and not just performing unchallenging, unappreciated tasks.

Secondly, the implications of the Hawthorne studies signaled the need for management to study and understand relationships among people. In these studies, as well as the many which followed, the most significant factor affecting organizational productivity was found to be the interpersonal relationships that are developed on the job, not just pay and working conditions. Mayo found that when informal groups identified with management, as they did at Hawthorne through the interview program, productivity rose. The increased productivity seemed to reflect the workers' feelings of competence—a sense of mastery over the job and work environment. Mayo also discovered that when the group felt that their own goals were in opposition to those of management, as often happened in situations where the workers were closely supervised and had no significant control over their job or environment, productivity remained at low levels or was even lowered.

These findings were important because they helped answer many of the questions that had puzzled management about why some groups seemed to be high producers while others hovered at a minimal level of output. The findings also encouraged management to involve workers in planning, organizing, and controlling their own work in an effort to secure their positive cooperation.

Mayo saw the development of informal groups as an indictment of an entire society which treated human beings as insensitive machines which were concerned only with economic self-interest. As a result, workers had been taught to look at work merely as an impersonal exchange of money for labor. Work in American industry meant humiliation—the performance of routine, tedious, and oversimplified tasks in an environment over which one had no control. This environment denied satisfaction of esteem and self-actualization needs on the job. Instead only physiological and security needs were satisfied. The lack of avenues for satisfying other needs led to tension, anxiety, and frustration in workers. Such feelings of helplessness were called "anomie" by Mayo. This condition was characterized by workers' feeling unimportant, confused, and unattached—victims of their own environment.

While anomie was a creation of the total society, Mayo felt its most extreme application was found in industrial settings where management held certain negative assumptions about the nature of man. According to Mayo, too many managers assumed that society consisted of a horde or mob of unorganized individuals whose only concern was self-preservation or self-interest. It was assumed that people were primarily dominated by physiological and security needs, wanting to make as much money as they could for as little work as possible. Thus, management operated and organized work on the basic assumption that workers, on the whole, were a contemptible lot. Mayo called this assumption the "Rabble Hypothesis." [26] He deplored the authoritarian, task-oriented management practices which it created.

THEORY X AND THEORY Y
Douglas McGregor

The work of Mayo and particularly his exposure of the Rabble Hypothesis may have paved the way for the development of the now classic "Theory X—Theory Y" by Douglas McGregor.[27] According to McGregor, traditional organization with its centralized decision-making, superior-subordinate pyramid, and external control of work is based upon assumptions about human nature and human motivation. These assumptions are very similar to the view of man defined by Mayo in the Rabble Hypothesis. Theory X assumes that most people prefer to be directed, are not interested in assuming responsibility, and want security above all. Accompanying this philosophy is the belief that people are motivated by money, fringe benefits, and the threat of punishment.

Managers who accept Theory X assumptions, attempt to structure, control, and closely supervise their employees. These managers feel that external control is clearly appropriate for dealing with unreliable, irresponsible, and immature people.

After describing Theory X, McGregor questioned whether this view of man is correct and if management practices based upon it are appropriate in many situations today: Isn't man in a democratic society, with its increasing level of education and standard of living, capable of more mature behavior? Drawing heavily on Maslow's hierarchy of needs, McGregor concluded that Theory X assumptions about the nature of man are generally inaccurate and that management approaches which develop from these assumptions will often fail to motivate individuals to work toward organizational goals. Management by direction and control may not succeed, according to McGregor, because it is a questionable method for motivating people whose physiological and safety needs are reasonably satisfied and whose affiliation, esteem, and self-actualization needs are becoming predominant.

McGregor felt that management needed practices based on a more accurate understanding of the nature of man and human motivation. As a result of his feeling, McGregor developed an alternate theory of human behavior called Theory Y. This theory assumes that people are *not,* by nature, lazy and unreliable. It postulates that man can be basically self-directed and creative at work if properly motivated. Therefore, it should be an essential task of management to unleash this potential in man. The properly motivated worker can achieve his own goals *best* by directing *his own* efforts toward accomplishing organizational goals.

Theory X	*Theory Y*
1. Work is inherently distasteful to most people.	1. Work is as natural as play, if the conditions are favorable.
2. Most people are not ambitious, have little desire for responsibility, and prefer to be directed.	2. Self-control is often indispensable in achieving organizational goals.
3. Most people have little capacity for creativity in solving organizational problems.	3. The capacity for creativity in solving organizational problems is widely distributed in the population.
4. Motivation occurs only at the physiological and security levels.	4. Motivation occurs at the affiliation, esteem, and self-actualization levels, as well as physiological and security levels.
5. Most people must be closely controlled and often coerced to achieve organizational objectives.	5. People can be self-directed and creative at work if properly motivated.

TABLE 3.1 List of assumptions about nature of man which underline McGregor's Theory X and Theory Y.

Managers who accept the Theory Y image of human nature, do *not* usually structure, control, or closely supervise the work environment for employees. Instead, they attempt to help their employees mature by exposing them to progressively less external control, allowing them to assume more and more self-control. Employees are able to achieve the satisfaction of affiliation, esteem, and self-actualization needs within this kind of environment, often neglected on the job. To the extent that the job does not provide need satisfaction at every level, today's employee will usually look elsewhere for significant need satisfaction. This helps explain some of the current problems management is facing in such areas as turnover and absenteeism. McGregor argues that this does not have to be the case.

Management is interested in work and McGregor feels work is as natural and can be as satisfying for people as play. After all, both work and play are physical and mental activity; consequently, there is no inherent difference between work and play. In reality though, particularly under Theory X management, a distinct difference in need satisfaction is discernible. Whereas play is internally controlled by the individual (he decides what he wants to do) work is externally controlled by others (the worker has no control over his job). Thus, management and its assumptions about the nature of man have built in a difference between work and play which seems unnatural. As a result, people are stifled at work, and hence, look for excuses to spend more and more time away from the job in order to satisfy their esteem and self-actualization needs (provided they have enough money to satisfy their physiological and safety needs). Because of their conditioning to Theory X types of management, most employees consider work a *necessary evil* rather than a source of personal challenge and satisfaction.

Does work really have to be a necessary evil? No—especially in organizations where cohesive work groups have developed and where the goals of groups parallel organizational goals. In such organizations, there is high productivity and people come to work gladly because work is inherently satisfying.

IMMATURITY-MATURITY THEORY
Chris Argyris

Even though management based on the assumptions of Theory X is perhaps no longer appropriate in the opinion of McGregor and others, it is still widely practiced. Consequently, a large majority of the people in the United States today are treated as immature human beings in their working environments. It is this fact that has produced many of our current organizational problems. Chris Argyris of Yale University has examined industrial organizations to determine what effect management practices have had on individual behavior and personal growth within the work environment.[28]

According to Argyris, there are seven changes which should take place in the personality of an individual if he is to develop into a mature person over the years:

First, an individual moves from a passive state as an infant, to a state of increasing activity as an adult. Second, an individual develops from a state of dependency upon others as an infant to a state of relative independence as an adult. Third, an individual behaves in only a few ways as an infant, but as an adult, he is capable of behaving in many ways. Fourth, an individual has erratic, casual, and shallow interests as an infant, but develops deeper and stronger interests as an adult. Fifth, a child's time perspective is very short, involving only the present, but as he matures, his time perspective increases to include the past and the future. Sixth, an individual as an infant is subordinate to everyone, but he moves to equal or superior position with others as an adult. Seventh, as a child, an individual lacks an awareness of a "self," but as an adult, he is not only aware of, but he is able to control this. Argyris postulates that these changes reside on a continuum and that the "healthy" personality develops along the continuum from "immaturity" or "maturity."

IMMATURITY ⟶ MATURITY	
passive — — — — — — — — — — — — — — — —	increased activity
dependence — — — — — — — — — — — — — — —	independence
behave in a few ways — — — — — — — — — — — —	capable of behaving in many ways
erratic shallow interests — — — — — — — — — —	deeper and stronger interests
short time perspective — — — — — — — — — — —	long time perspective (past and future)
subordinate position — — — — — — — — — — — —	equal or superordinate position
lack of awareness of self — — — — — — — — — —	awareness and control over self

TABLE 3.2 Immaturity—maturity continuum.

These changes are only general tendencies, but give some light to the matter of maturity. Norms of the individual's culture and personality inhibit and limit maximum expression and growth of the adult, yet the tendency is to move toward the "maturity" end of the continuum with age. Argyris would be the first to admit that few, if any, develop to full maturity.

In examining the widespread worker apathy and lack of effort in industry, Argyris questions whether these problems are simply the result of individual laziness. He suggests that this is *not* the case. Argyris contends that, in many cases, when people join the work force, they are kept from maturing by the management practices utilized in their organizations. In these organizations, they are given minimal control over their environment and are encouraged to be passive, dependent, and subordinate; therefore, they behave immaturely. The worker in many organizations is expected to act in immature ways rather than as a mature adult.

According to Argyris, keeping people immature is built into the very nature of the formal organization. He argues that because organizations are usually created to achieve goals or objectives that can best be met collectively, the formal organization is often the architect's conception of how these objectives may be achieved. In this sense the individual is fitted to the job. The design comes first. This design is based upon four concepts of scientific management: task specialization, chain of command, unity of direction, and span of control. Management tries to increase and enhance organizational and administrative efficiency and productivity by making workers "interchangeable parts."

Basic to these concepts is that power and authority should rest in the hands of a few at the top of the organization, and thus, those at the lower end of the chain of command are strictly controlled by their superiors or the system itself. Task specialization often results in the over-simplification of the job so that it becomes repetitive, routine, and unchallenging. This implies directive, task-oriented leadership where decisions about the work are made by the superior with the workers only carrying out those decisions. This type of leadership evokes managerial controls such as budgets, some incentive systems, time and motion studies, and standard operating procedures which can restrict the initiative and creativity of workers.

Argyris feels that these concepts of formal organization lead to assumptions about human nature that are incompatible with the proper development of maturity in human personality. He sees a definite incongruity between the needs of a mature personality and formal organizations as they now exist. Since he implies that the classical theory of management (based on Theory X assumptions) usually prevails, management creates child-like roles for workers which frustrate any natural development.

An example of how work is often designed at this extremely low level was dramatically illustrated by the successful use of mentally retarded workers in such jobs. Argyris cites two instances, one in a knitting mill and the other in a radio manufacturing corporation in which mentally retarded people were successfully employed on unskilled jobs. In both cases, the managers praised these workers for their excellent performance. In fact, a manager in the radio corporation reported:

> The girls proved to be exceptionally well-behaved, particularly obedient, and strictly honest and trustworthy. They carried out work required of them to such a degree of efficiency that *we were surprised they were classed as subnormals for their age.* Their attendance was good, and their behavior was, if anything, certainly better than that of any other employee of the same age.[29]

Disturbed by what he finds in many organizations, Argyris, as did McGregor, challenges management to provide a work climate in which everyone has a chance to grow and mature as an individual, as a member of a group by satisfying his own needs, while working for the success of the organization. Implicit here is the belief that man can be basically self-directed and creative at work if properly motivated, and, therefore, management based on the assumption of Theory Y will be more profitable for the individual and the organization.

More and more companies are starting to listen to the challenge that Argyris is directing at management. For example, the president of a large company asked Argyris to show him how to better motivate his workers. Together they went into one of his production plants where a product similar to a radio was being assembled. There were twelve girls involved in assembling the product, each doing a small segment of the job as designed by an industrial engineer. The group also had a foreman, an inspector, and a packer.

Argyris proposed a one-year experiment during which each of the girls would assemble the total product in a manner of their own choice. At the same time they would inspect, sign their name to the product, pack it, and handle any correspondence involving complaints about it. The girls were assured that they would receive no cut in pay if production dropped but would receive more pay if production increased.

Once the experiment began, production dropped 70 per cent during the first month. By the end of six weeks it was even worse. The girls were upset, morale was down. This continued until the eighth week, when production started to rise. By the end of the fifteenth week production was higher than it had ever been before. And this was without an inspector, packer, or industrial engineer. More important than increased productivity, costs due to errors and waste decreased 94 per cent; letters of complaint dropped 96 per cent.

Experiments like this are being duplicated in numerous other situations. It is being found over and over again that broadening individual responsibility is beneficial to both the workers and the company. Giving people the opportunity to grow and mature on the job helps them satisfy more than just physiological and safety needs, which, in turn, motivates them and allows them to use more of their potential in accomplishing organizational goals. While all workers do *not* want to accept more responsibility or deal with the added problems responsibility inevitably brings, Argyris contends that the number of employees whose motivation can be improved by increasing and upgrading their responsibility is much larger than most managers would suspect.

MOTIVATION-HYGIENE THEORY
Frederick Herzberg

As people mature, we have noted that needs such as esteem and self-actualization seem to become more important. One of the most interesting series of studies which concentrates heavily on these areas are those being directed by Frederick Herzberg of Case Western Reserve University.[30] Out of these studies has developed a theory of work motivation which has broad implications for management and its efforts toward effective utilization of human resources.

Herzberg, in developing his motivation-hygiene theory, seemed to sense that scholars like McGregor and Argyris were touching on something important. Knowledge about the nature of man, his motives and needs, could be invaluable to organizations and individuals.

> To industry, the payoff for a study of job attitudes would be increased productivity, decreased absenteeism, and smoother working relations. To the individual, an understanding of the forces that lead to improved morale would bring greater happiness and greater self-realization.[31]

Herzberg set out to collect data on job attitudes from which assumptions about human behavior could be made. The motivation-hygiene theory resulted from the analysis of an initial study by Herzberg and his colleagues at the Psychological Service of Pittsburgh. This study involved extensive interviews with some 200 engineers and accountants from eleven industries in the Pittsburgh area. In the interviews, they were asked about what kinds of things on their job made them unhappy or dissatisfied and what things made them happy or satisfied.

In analyzing the data from these interviews, Herzberg concluded that man has two different categories of needs which are essentially independent of each other and affect behavior in different ways. He found that when people felt dissatisfied about their jobs, they were concerned about the environment in which they were working. On the other hand, when people felt good about their jobs, this had to do with the work itself. Herzberg called the first category of needs *hygiene factors* because they describe man's environment and serve the primary function of preventing job dissatisfaction. He called the second category of needs *motivators* since they seemed to be effective in motivating people to superior performance.

Hygiene Factors

Company policies and administration, supervision, working conditions, interpersonal relations, money, status, and security may be thought of as hygiene factors. These are not an intrinsic part of a job, but are related to the conditions under which a job is performed. Herzberg relates his use of the word "hygiene" to its medical meaning (preventative and environmental). Hygiene factors produce no growth in worker output capacity; they only prevent losses in worker performance due to work restriction.

Motivators

Satisfying factors that involve feelings of achievement, professional growth, and recognition that one can experience in a job which offers challenge and scope are referred to as motivators. Herzberg used this term because these factors seem capable of having a positive effect on job satisfaction often resulting in an increase in one's total output capacity.

HYGIENE FACTORS	MOTIVATORS
Environment	*The Job Itself*
Policies and administration	Achievement
Supervision	Recognition for accomplishment
Working conditions	Challenging work
Interpersonal relations	Increased responsibility
Money, status, security	Growth and development

TABLE 3.3   Motivation and hygiene factors.

Herzberg's framework seems compatible with Maslow's hierarchy of needs. By integrating the two as illustrated in Figure 3.1, we can show certain similarities between an individual's motivation and ability and its effects on performance.

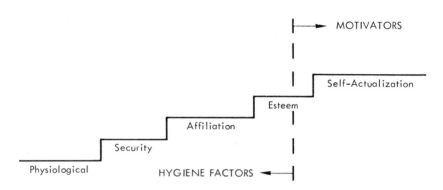

FIGURE 3.1   The relationships between the motivation-hygiene theory and Maslow's hierarchy of needs.

We feel that the physiological, security, affiliation, and part of the esteem needs are all hygiene factors. The esteem needs are divided because there are some distinct differences between status per se and recognition. Status tends to be a function of the position one occupies. One may have gained this position through family ties or social pressures, and thus this position is not a reflection of personal achievement or earned recognition. Recognition is gained through competence and achievement. It is earned and granted by others. Consequently, status is classified with physiological, security, and affiliation needs as a hygiene factor, while recognition is classified with self-actualization as a motivator.

Perhaps an example will further differentiate between hygiene factors and motivators. This might help explain the reason for classifying needs as Herzberg has done as well as in a hierarchical arrangement.

Let us assume that a man is highly motivated and is working at 90 per cent of capacity. He has a good working relationship with his supervisor, is well satisfied with his pay and working conditions, and is part of a congenial work group. Suppose his supervisor is suddenly transferred and replaced by a person he is unable to work with, or he finds out that someone whose work he feels is inferior to his own is receiving more pay. How do these factors affect a man's behavior? Since we know performance or productivity depends on both ability and motivation, these unsatisfied hygiene needs (supervision and money) may lead to restriction of output. In some cases this is intentional while in others the individual may not be consciously aware that he is holding back. In either case, though, productivity will be lowered as illustrated in Figure 3.2.

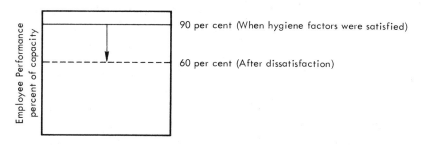

FIGURE 3.2   Effect of dissatisfying hygienes.

In this illustration, even if his former supervisor returns and his salary is readjusted well above his expectations, his productivity will probably increase only to its original level.

Conversely, let us take the same person and assume that dissatisfaction had not occurred; he is working at 90 per cent capacity. Suppose he is given an opportunity to mature and satisfy his motivational needs in an environment where he is free to exercise some initiative and creativity, to make decisions, to handle problems, and to take responsibility. What effect will this situation have on this individual? If he is able to successfully fulfill his supervisor's expectations in performing these new responsibilities, he may still work at 90 per cent capacity, but as a person he may have matured and grown in his ability and may be capable now of more productivity as illustrated in Figure 3.3, page 50.

Hygiene needs, when satisfied, tend to eliminate dissatisfaction

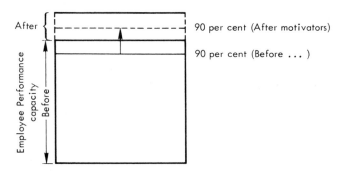

FIGURE 3.3   Effect of satisfying motivators.

and work restriction but do little to motivate an individual to superior performance or increased capacity. Satisfaction of the motivators, however, will permit an individual to grow and develop in a mature way, often implementing an increase in ability. Herzberg encourages management to design into the work environment an opportunity to satisfy the motivators.

Prior to Herzberg's work, many other behavioral scientists were concerned with worker motivation. For several years there was an emphasis on what was termed "job enlargement." This was purported to be an answer to the overspecialization which had characterized many industrial organizations. The assumption was that a worker could gain more satisfaction at work if his job was enlarged, that is, if the number of operations in which he engaged was increased.

Herzberg makes some astute observations about this trend. He claims that doing a snippet of this and a snippet of that does not necessarily result in motivation. Washing dishes, then silverware, then pots and pans does no more to satisfy and provide an opportunity to grow than washing only dishes. What we really need to do with work, Herzberg suggests, is to *enrich* the job. By job enrichment is meant the deliberate upgrading of responsibility, scope, and challenge in work.

Example of Job Enrichment

An example of job enrichment may be illustrated by the experience an industrial relations superintendent had with a group of janitors. When the superintendent was transferred to a new plant, he soon found, much to his amazement, that in addition to his duties, fifteen janitors in plant maintenance reported directly to him. There was no foreman over these men. Upon browsing through the files one day, the superintendent noticed there was a history of complaints about housekeeping around the plant. After talking to others and observing for himself, it took the superintendent little time to confirm the reports. The janitors seemed to be lazy, unreliable, and generally unmotivated. They were walking examples of Theory X assumptions about human nature.

Determined to do something about the behavior of the janitors, the superintendent called a group meeting of all fifteen men. He opened the meeting by saying that he understood there were a number of housekeeping problems in the plant, but confessed that he didn't know what to do about them. Since he felt they, as janitors, were experts in the housekeeping area, he asked if together they would help him solve these problems. "Does anyone have a suggestion?" he asked. There was a deadly silence. The superintendent sat down and said nothing; the janitors said nothing. This lasted for almost twenty minutes. Finally one janitor spoke up and related a problem he was having in his area and made a suggestion. Soon others joined in, and suddenly the janitors were involved in a lively discussion while the superintendent listened and jotted down their ideas. At the conclusion of the meeting the suggestions were summarized with tacit acceptance by all, including the superintendent.

After the meeting, the superintendent referred any housekeeping problems to the janitors, individually or as a group. For example, when any cleaning equipment or material salesmen came to the plant the superintendent did not talk to them, the janitors did. In fact, the janitors were given an office where they could talk to salesmen. In addition, regular meetings continued to be held where problems and ideas were discussed.

All of this had a tremendous influence on the behavior of these men. They developed a cohesive productive team that took pride in its work. Even their appearance changed. Once a grubby lot, now they appeared at work in clean, pressed work clothes. All over the plant, people were amazed how clean and well-kept everything had become. The superintendent was continually stopped by supervisors in the plant and asked, "What have you done to those lazy, good-for-nothing janitors, given them pep pills?" Even the superintendent could not believe his eyes. It was not uncommon to see one or two janitors running floor tests to see which wax or cleaner did the best job. Since they had to make all the decisions including committing funds for their supplies, they wanted to know which were the best. Such activities, while taking time, did not distract from their work. In fact, these men worked harder and more efficiently than ever before in their lives.

This example illustrates that even at low levels in an organization, people can respond in responsible and productive ways to a work environment in which they are given an opportunity to grow and mature. People begin to satisfy their esteem and self-actualization needs by participating in the planning, organizing, motivating, and controlling of their own tasks.

MANAGEMENT SYSTEMS
Rensis Likert

Most managers, if asked what they would do if they suddenly lost half of their plant, equipment or capital resources, are quick to answer. Insurance or borrowing are often avenues open to refurbish plant, equipment, or capital. Yet when these same managers are asked what they would do if they suddenly lost half of their human resources —managers, supervisors, and hourly employees—they are at a loss for words. There is no insurance against outflows of human resources. Recruiting, training, and developing large numbers of new personnel into a working team takes years. In a competitive environment this is almost an impossible task. Organizations are only beginning to realize that their most important assets are human resources and that the managing of these resources is one of their most crucial tasks.

Rensis Likert and his colleagues of the Institute for Social Research at the University of Michigan have emphasized the need to consider both human resources and capital resources as assets requiring proper management.[32] As a result of behavioral research studies of numerous organizations, Likert is now implementing organizational change programs in various industrial settings. It appears these programs are intended to help organizations move from Theory X to Theory Y assumptions, from fostering immature behavior to encouraging and developing mature behavior, from emphasizing only hygiene factors to recognizing and helping workers to satisfy the motivators.

Likert in his studies has found that the prevailing management styles of organization can be depicted on a continuum from System 1 through System 4. These systems might be described as follows.

System 1—Management is seen as having no confidence or trust in subordinates since they are seldom involved in any aspect of the decision-making process. The bulk of the decisions and the goal setting of the organization are made at the top and issued down the chain of command. Subordinates are forced to work with fear, threats, punishment, and occasional rewards and need satisfaction at the physiological and safety levels. The little superior-subordinate interaction which does take place is usually with fear and mistrust. While the control process is highly concentrated in top management, an informal organization generally develops which opposes the goals of the formal organization.

System 2—Management is seen as having condescending confidence and trust in subordinates such as master has toward servant. While the bulk of the decisions and goal setting of the organization are made at the top, many decisions are made within a prescribed framework at lower levels. Rewards and some actual or potential punishment are used to motivate workers. Any superior-subordinate interaction takes place with some condescension by superiors and fear and caution by subordinates. While the control process is still concentrated in top management, some is delegated to middle and lower levels. An informal organization usually develops but it does not always resist formal organizational goals.

System 3—Management is seen as having substantial but not complete confidence and trust in subordinates. While broad policy and general decisions are kept at the top, subordinates are permitted to make more specific decisions at lower levels. Communication flows both up and down the hierarchy. Rewards, occasional punishment, and some involvement are used to motivate workers. There is a moderate amount of superior-subordinate interaction, often with a fair amount of confidence and trust. Significant aspects of the control process are delegated downward with a feeling of responsibility at both higher and lower levels. An informal organization may develop but it may either support or partially resist goals of the organization.

System 4—Management is seen as having complete confidence and trust in subordinates. Decision-making is widely dispersed throughout the organization, although well integrated. Communication flows not only up and down the hierarchy but among peers. Workers are motivated by participation and involvement in developing economic rewards, setting goals, improving methods and appraising progress toward goals. There is extensive, friendly superior-subordinate interaction with a high degree of confidence and trust. There is widespread responsibility for the control process, with the lower units fully involved. The informal and formal organizations are often one and the same. Thus, all social forces support efforts to achieve stated organizational goals.[33]

In summary, System 1 is a task-oriented, highly structured authoritarian management style, while System 4 is a relationships-oriented management style based on teamwork, mutual trust, and confidence. Systems 2 and 3 are intermediate stages between two extremes which approximate closely Theory X and Theory Y assumptions.

To expedite the analysis of a company's present behavior, Likert's group developed an instrument which enables members to rate their organization in terms of its management system. This instrument is designed to gather data about a number of operating characteristics of an organization. These characteristics include leadership, motivation, communication, decision making, interaction and influence, goal setting, and the control process used by the organization. Sample items from this instrument are presented in Figure 3.4. The complete instrument includes over twenty such items.[34]

In testing this instrument, Likert asked hundreds of managers from many different organizations to indicate where the *most* productive department, division, or organization they have known would fall between System 1 and System 4. Then these same managers were asked to repeat this process and indicate the position of the *least* productive department, division, or organization they have known. While the ratings of the most and least productive departments varied among managers, almost without exception each manager rated the high-producing unit closer to System 4 than the low-producing department. In summary, Likert has found that the closer the management style of an organization approaches System 4, the more likely it is to have a continuous record of high productivity. Similarly, the closer this style reflects System 1, the more likely it is to have a sustained record of low productivity.

Likert has also used this instrument to measure, not only what an individual believes are the present characteristics of his organization but also to find out what he would like these characteristics to be. Data generated from this use of the instrument with managers of well-known companies has indicated a large discrepancy between the management system they feel their company is now using and the management system they feel would be most appropriate. System 4 is seen as being most appropriate, but few see their companies presently utilizing this approach. These implications have led to attempts by

Organizational variable	System 1	System 2	System 3	System 4
Leadership processes used Extent to which superiors have confidence and trust in subordinates	Have no confidence and trust in subordinates	Have condescending confidence and trust, such as master has to servant	Substantial but not complete confidence and trust; still wishes to keep control of decisions	Complete confidence and trust in all matters
Character of motivational forces Manner in which motives are used	Fear, threats, punishment, and occasional rewards	Rewards and some actual or potential punishment	Rewards, occasional punishment, and some involvement	Economic rewards based on compensation system developed through participation; group participation and involvement in setting goals, improving methods, appraising progress toward goals, etc.
Character of interaction-influence process Amount and character of interaction	Little interaction and always with fear and distrust	Little interaction and usually with some condescension by superiors; fear and caution by subordinates	Moderate interaction, often with fair amount of confidence and trust	Extensive, friendly interaction with high degree of confidence and trust

FIGURE 3.4 Examples of items from Likert's table of organizational and performance characteristics of different management systems.

some organizations to adapt their management system to more closely approximate System 4. Changes of this kind are not easy. They involve a massive re-education of all concerned from the top management to hourly workers.

Theory into Practice

One instance of a successful change in the management style of an organization occurred with a leading firm in the pajama industry.[35] After being unprofitable for several years this company was purchased by another corporation. At the time of the transaction, the purchased company was using a management style falling between System 1 and System 2. Some major changes were soon implemented by the new owners. The changes that were put into effect included extensive modifications in how the work was organized, improved maintenance of machinery, and a training program involving managers and workers at every level. Managers and supervisors were exposed in depth to the philosophy and understanding of management approaching System 4. All of these changes were supported by the top management of the purchasing company.

Although productivity dropped in the first several months after the initiation of the change program, productivity had increased by almost 30 per cent within two years. Although it is not possible to calculate exactly how much of the increased productivity resulted from the change in management system, it was obvious to the researchers that the impact was considerable. In addition to increases in productivity, manufacturing costs decreased 20 per cent, turnover was cut almost in half, and morale rose considerably (reflecting a more friendly attitude of workers toward the organization). The company's image in the community was enhanced and for the first time in years the company began to show a profit.

SUMMARY AND CONCLUSION

We have tried through the material presented to examine what is known today about understanding and motivating employees. The attempt has been to review theoretical literature, empirical research and case examples with the intention of integrating these sources into frameworks which may be useful to managers for analyzing and understanding behavior. Analyzing and understanding are necessary but the real value of the application of the behavioral sciences will be their usefulness in directing, changing, and controlling behavior. Beginning with Chapter Four a framework for applying leader behavior will be presented.

IV

Leader Behavior

The successful organization has one major attribute that sets it apart from unsuccessful organizations: dynamic and effective leadership. Peter F. Drucker points out that managers (business leaders) are the basic and scarcest resource of any business enterprise.[36] Statistics from recent years make this point more evident: "Of every 100 new business establishments started, approximately 50, or one half go out of business within two years. By the end of five years, only one third of the original 100 will still be in business." [37] Most of the failures can be attributed to ineffective leadership.

On all sides there is an almost frenzied search for persons who have the necessary ability to enable them to lead effectively. This shortage of effective leadership is not confined to business but is evident in the lack of able administrators in government, education, foundations, churches, and every other form of organization. Thus, when we decry the scarcity of leadership talent in our society, we are not talking about a lack of people to fill administrative or executive positions; we have plenty of administrative "bodies." What we are agonizing over is a scarcity of people who are willing to assume significant leadership roles in our society and can get the job done effectively.

LEADERSHIP DEFINED

According to George R. Terry, "Leadership is the activity of influencing people to strive willingly for group objectives."[38] Robert Tannenbaum, Irving R. Weschler and Fred Massarik define leadership as, "interpersonal influence exercised in a situation and directed, through the communication process, toward the attainment of a specialized goal or goals."[39] Harold Koontz and Cyril O'Donnell state that "leadership is *influencing* people to follow in the achievement of a common goal."[40]

A review of other writers reveals that most management writers agree that leadership is *the process of influencing the activities of an individual or a group in efforts toward goal achievement in a given situation.* From this definition of leadership, it follows that the leadership process is a function of the *leader,* the *follower,* and the *situation,* L = f(l,f,s).

TRAIT VS. SITUATIONAL APPROACH
TO THE STUDY OF LEADERSHIP

For many years the most common approach to the study of leadership concentrated on leadership traits per se, suggesting that there were certain qualities, such as physical energy or friendliness, that were essential for effective leadership. These inherent personal qualities, like intelligence, were felt to be transferable from one situation to another. Since all individuals did not have these qualities, only those who had them would be considered to be potential leaders. Consequently this approach seemed to question the value of training individuals to assume leadership positions. It implied that if we could discover how to identify and measure these leadership qualities (which are inborn in the individual), we should be able to screen leaders from nonleaders. Leadership training would then be helpful only to those with inherent leadership traits.

A review of the research literature using this trait approach to leadership has revealed few significant or consistent findings.[41] As Eugene E. Jennings concluded, "Fifty years of study have failed to produce one personality trait or set of qualities that can be used to discriminate leaders and non-leaders."[42] Empirical studies suggest that leadership is a dynamic process, varying from situation to situation with changes in leaders, followers, and situations. Current literature seems to support this situational or leader behavior approach to the study of leadership.[43]

The focus in the situational approach to leadership is on observed behavior, not on any hypothetical inborn or acquired ability or potential for leadership. The emphasis is on the behavior of leaders and their group members (followers) and various situations. With this emphasis upon behavior and environment, more encouragement is given to the possibility of training individuals in adapting styles of leader behavior to varying situations. Therefore it is believed that most people can increase their effectiveness in leadership roles through education, training, and development. From observations of the frequency (or infrequency) of certain leader behavior in numerous types of situations, theoretical models can be developed to help a leader make some predictions about the most appropriate leader behavior for his present situation. For these reasons, in this chapter we will talk in terms of leader behavior rather than leadership traits, thus emphasizing the situational approach to leadership.

LEADERSHIP PROCESS

We have defined leadership as the process of influencing the activities of an individual or a group in efforts toward goal achievement in a given situation. In essence, leadership involves accomplishing goals with and through people. Therefore a leader must be concerned about tasks and human relationships. Although using different terminology, Chester I. Barnard identified these same leadership concerns in his classic work, *The Functions of the Executive* in the late 1930's.[44] These leadership concerns seem to be a reflection of two of the earliest schools of thought in organizational theory—scientific management and human relations.

Scientific Management Movement

In the early 1900's one of the most widely read theorists on administration was Frederick Winslow Taylor. The basis for his *scientific management* was technological in nature. It was felt that the best way to increase output was to improve the techniques or methods used by workers. Consequently, he has been interpreted as considering people as instruments or machines to be manipulated by their leaders. Accepting this assumption, other theorists of the scientific management movement proposed that an organization as rationally planned and executed as possible be developed to create more efficiency in administration and consequently increase production. Management was to be divorced from human affairs and emotions. The result was that the people or workers had to adjust to the management and not the management to the people.

To accomplish this plan, Taylor initiated time and motion studies to analyze work tasks in order to improve performance in every aspect of the organization. Once jobs had been reorganized with efficiency in mind, the economic self-interest of the workers could be satisfied through various incentive work plans (piece rates, etc.).

The function of the leader under scientific management or classical theory was quite obviously to set up and enforce performance criteria to meet organizational goals. His main focus was on the needs of the organization and not on the needs of the individual.[45]

Human Relations Movement

In the 1920's and early 1930's, the trend initiated by Taylor was to be replaced at center stage by the *human relations* movement. This was initiated by Elton Mayo and his associates. These theorists argued that in addition to finding the best technological methods to improve output, it was beneficial to management to look into human affairs. It was claimed that the real power centers within an organization were the interpersonal relations which developed within the working unit. The study of these human relations was the most important consideration for management and the analysis of organization. The organization was to be developed around the workers and had to take into consideration human feelings and attitudes.[46]

The function of the leader under human relations theory was to facilitate cooperative goal attainment among his followers while providing opportunities for their personal growth and development. His main focus, contrary to scientific management theory, was on individual needs and not the needs of the organization.

In essence, then, the scientific management movement emphasized a concern for task, while the human relations movement stressed a concern for relationships (people). The recognition of these two concerns has characterized the writings on leadership ever since the conflict between the scientific management and human relations schools of thought became apparent.

Authoritarian-Democratic-Laissez Faire Leader Behavior

Past writers have felt that concern for task tends to be represented by authoritarian leader behavior while a concern for relationships is represented by democratic leader behavior. This feeling was popular because it was generally agreed that a leader influences his followers by either of two ways: (1) he can tell his followers what to do and how to do it, or (2) he can share his leadership responsibilities with his followers by involving them in the planning and execution of the task. The former is the traditional authoritarian style which emphasizes task concerns. The latter is the more nondirective democratic style which stresses the concern for human relationships.

The differences in the two styles of leader behavior are based on the assumptions the leader makes about the source of his power or authority and human nature. The authoritarian style of leader behavior is often based on the assumption that the leader's power is derived from the position he occupies and that man is innately lazy and unreliable (Theory X), whereas the democratic style assumes the leader's power is granted by the group he is to lead and that men can be basically self-directed and creative at work if properly motivated (Theory Y). As a result, in the authoritarian style, all policies are determined by the leader, while in the democratic style, policies are open for group discussion and decision.

There are, of course, a wide variety of styles of leader behavior between these two extremes. Robert Tannenbaum and Warren H. Schmidt depicted a broad range of styles on a continuum moving from very authoritarian leader behavior at one end to very democratic leader behavior at the other end [47] as illustrated in Figure 4.1.

Leaders whose behavior is observed to be at the authoritarian end of the continuum tend to be task-oriented and use their power to influence their followers while leaders whose behavior appears to be at the democratic end tend to be group-oriented and thus give their followers considerable freedom in their work. Often this continuum is extended beyond democratic leader behavior to include a laissez-faire style. This style of behavior permits the members of the group to do whatever they want to do. No policies or procedures are established. Everyone is let alone. No one attempts to influence anyone else. As is evident, this style is not included in the continuum of leader behavior illustrated in Figure 4.1. This was done because it was felt that in reality, a laissez-faire atmosphere represents an absence of leadership.

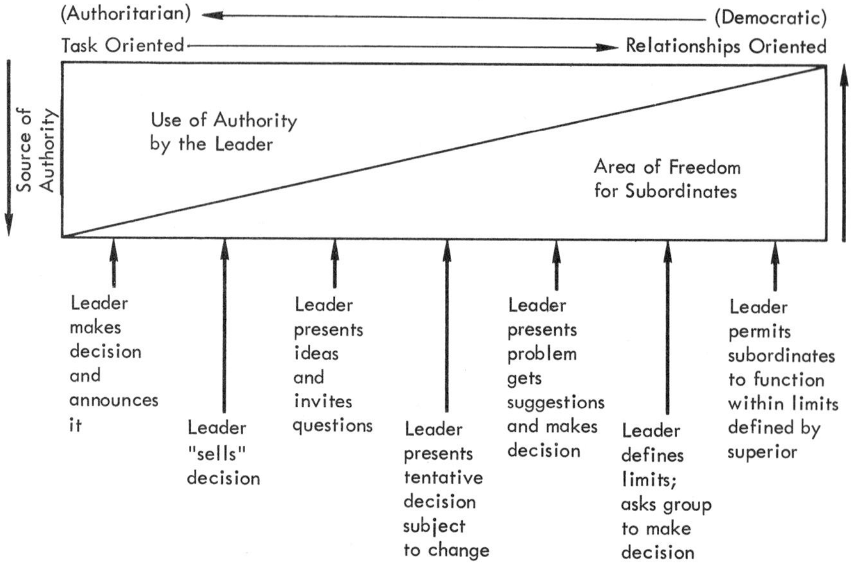
(Authoritarian)
(Democratic)
Task Oriented
Relationships Oriented
Source of Authority
Use of Authority by the Leader
Area of Freedom for Subordinates
Leader makes decision and announces it
Leader "sells" decision
Leader presents ideas and invites questions
Leader presents tentative decision subject to change
Leader presents problem gets suggestions and makes decision
Leader defines limits; asks group to make decision
Leader permits subordinates to function within limits defined by superior

FIGURE 4.1 Continuum of leader behavior.

The leadership role has been abdicated and therefore no leader behavior is being exhibited.

In recent years, research findings indicate that leadership styles vary considerably from leader to leader. Some leaders emphasize the task and can be described as authoritarian leaders while others stress interpersonal relationships and may be viewed as democratic leaders. Still others seem to be both task and relationships oriented. There are even some individuals in leadership positions who are not concerned about either. No dominant style appears. Instead various combinations are evident. Thus task-orientation and relationships-orientation are not either/or leadership concerns as the preceding continuum suggests. These concerns are separate and distinct dimensions which can be plotted on two separate axes, rather than a single continuum.

Ohio State Leadership Studies

The leadership studies initiated in 1945 by the Bureau of Business Research at Ohio State University attempted to identify dimensions of leader behavior through the development of the Leader Behavior

Description Questionnaire.[48] This instrument was designed to describe *how* a leader carries out his activities.

The staff, defining leadership as the behavior of an individual when he is directing the activities of a group toward a goal attainment, eventually narrowed the description of leader behavior to two dimensions: *initiating structure* and *consideration*. Initiating structure refers to "the leader's behavior in delineating the relationship between himself and members of the work-group and in endeavoring to establish well-defined patterns of organization, channels of communication, and methods of procedure." On the other hand, consideration refers to "behavior indicative of friendship, mutual trust, respect, and warmth in the relationship between the leader and the members of his staff." [49]

Initiating structure seems to be task-oriented. This dimension emphasizes the needs of the organization. At the same time consideration is relationships-oriented and tends to emphasize the needs of the individual.

In studying leader behavior the Ohio State staff found that initiating structure and consideration were separate and distinct dimensions. Thus it was during these studies that leader behavior was first plotted on two separate axes, rather than a single continuum. Four quadrants were developed to show various combinations of initiating structure (task) and consideration (relationships)—see Figure 4.2.

Michigan Leadership Studies

Occurring almost simultaneously with the Ohio State Leadership Studies were the early studies of the Survey Research Center at the University of Michigan.[50] The attempt there was to approach the study of leadership by locating clusters of characteristics which seemed to be related to each other and tests of effectiveness. The studies identified two concepts which they called *employee orientation* and *production orientation*.

A leader who is described as employee-oriented stresses the relationships aspect of his job. He feels that every employee is important. He takes interest in everyone, accepting their individuality and personal needs. Production orientation emphasizes production and the technical aspects of the job, viewing employees as tools to accomplish the goals of the organization. These two orientations parallel the Ohio State Leadership dimensions of initiating structure and consideration.

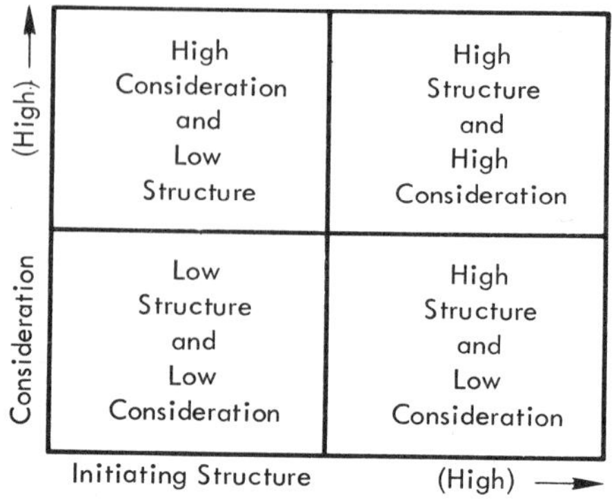
High
Consideration
and
Low
Structure
High
Structure
and
High
Consideration
Low
Structure
and
Low
Consideration
High
Structure
and
Low
Consideration
Consideration
(High)
Initiating Structure
(High)

FIGURE 4.2 The Ohio State leadership quadrants.

Group Dynamics Studies

Dorwin Cartwright and Alvin Zander, based on the findings of numerous studies at the Research Center for Group Dynamics, claim that all group objectives fall into one of two categories: (1) the achievement of some specific group goal, or (2) the maintenance or strengthening of the group itself.[51]

According to Cartwright and Zander, the type of behavior involved in goal achievement is illustrated by these examples: The manager "initiates action . . . keeps members' attention on the goal . . . clarifies the issue and develops a procedural plan." [52]

On the other hand, characteristic behaviors for group maintenance are: The manager "keeps interpersonal relations pleasant . . . arbitrates disputes . . . provides encouragement . . . gives the minority a chance to be heard . . . stimulates self-direction . . . and increases the interdependence among members." [53]

Goal achievement seems to coincide with the task concepts discussed earlier (initiating structure and production orientation), while group maintenance parallels the relationships concepts (consideration and employee orientation).

Managerial Grid

In discussing the Ohio State, Michigan, and Group Dynamics Leadership studies, we have been concentrating on two theoretical concepts. Robert R. Blake and Jane S. Mouton have popularized these concepts in their Managerial Grid and have used them extensively in organization and management development programs.[54]

In the Managerial Grid, five different types of leadership based on concern for production (task) and concern for people (relationships) are located in the four quadrants identified by the Ohio State studies.

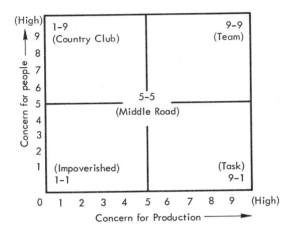

FIGURE 4.3 The Managerial Grid leadership styles.

Concern for production is illustrated on the horizontal axis. Production becomes more important to the leader as his rating advances on the horizontal scale. A leader with a rating of 9 on the horizontal axis has a maximum concern for production.

Concern for people is illustrated on the vertical axis. People become more important to the leader as his rating progresses up the vertical axis. A leader with a rating of 9 on the vertical axis has maximum concern for people.

The five leadership styles are described as follows:

Impoverished—Exertion of minimum effort to get required work done is appropriate to sustain organization membership.

Country Club—Thoughtful attention to needs of people for satisfying relationships leads to a comfortable friendly organization atmosphere and work tempo.

Task—Efficiency in operations results from arranging conditions of work in such a way that human elements interfere to a minimum degree.

Middle-of-the-Road—Adequate organization performance is possible through balancing the necessity to get out work while maintaining morale of people at a satisfactory level.

Team—Work accomplishment is from committed people; interdependence through a "common stake" in organization purpose leads to relationships of trust and respect.[55]

In essence, the Managerial Grid has given popular terminology to five points within the four quadrants of the Ohio State studies. A diagram combining the two theories could be illustrated as shown in Figure 4.4.

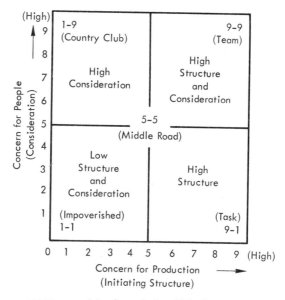

FIGURE 4.4   Merging of the Ohio State and the Managerial Grid theories of leadership.

IS THERE A BEST STYLE OF LEADERSHIP?

After identifying the two central concerns of any leadership situation, task and relationships, the researchers discussed earlier have recognized the potential conflict in satisfying both concerns. Consequently, an attempt has been made to find a middle ground which will encompass both concerns. Chester Barnard recognized this fact when he purposely included both concerns as necessary factors for the survival of any organization.[56]

According to Warren G. Bennis, theorists like Barnard who express concern for both task and relationships are called "revisionists."

> The revisionists are now concerned with external, economic factors, with productivity, with formal status, and so on, but not to the exclusion of the human elements that the traditional theorists so neglected. So what we are observing now is the pendulum swinging just a little farther to the middle from its once extreme position to balance and modulate with more refinement in the human organization requirements.[57]

Andrew W. Halpin, using the Leader Behavior Description Questionnaire in a study of school superintendents, found that the administrators he interviewed had a tendency to view consideration and initiating structure as either/or forms of leader behavior. "Some administrators act as if they were forced to emphasize one form of behavior at the expense of the other." [58] Halpin stressed that this conflict between initiating structure and consideration should not necessarily exist. He points out that according to his findings, "effective or desirable leadership behavior is characterized by high scores on both Initiating Structure and Consideration. Conversely, ineffective or undesirable leadership behavior is marked by low scores on both dimensions." [59]

From these observations, Halpin concludes that a successful leader, "must contribute to both major group objectives: goal achievement and group maintenance (in Cartwright and Zander's terms); or in Barnard's terms, he must facilitate cooperative group action that is both effective and efficient." [60] Thus the Ohio State Leadership studies seem to conclude that the high consideration and initiating structure style is theoretically the ideal or "best" leader behavior, while the style low on both dimensions is theoretically the "worst."

The Managerial Grid also implies that the most desirable leader behavior is "team management" (maximum concern for production and people). In fact, Blake and Mouton have developed training programs to change managers toward a 9-9 management style.[61]

Using the earlier Michigan Studies as a starting place, Rensis Likert did some extensive research to discover the general pattern of management used by high-producing managers in contrast to that used by the other managers. He found that: "Supervisors with the best records of performance focus their primary attention on the human aspects of their subordinates' problems and on endeavoring to build effective work groups with high performance goals." [62] These supervisors were called "employee-centered." Other supervisors who kept constant pressure on production were called "job-centered" and were found more often to have low-producing sections.[63] Figure 4.5 presents the findings from one study.

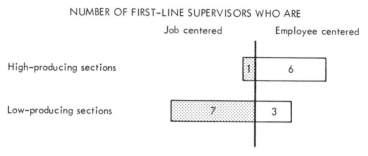

FIGURE 4.5 Employee-centered supervisors are higher producers than job-centered supervisors.

Likert also discovered that high-producing supervisors "make clear to their subordinates what the objectives are and what needs to be accomplished and then give them freedom to do the job." [64] Thus he found that general, rather than close, supervision tended to be associated with high productivity. This relationship, found in a study of clerical workers,[65] is illustrated in Figure 4.6.

The implication throughout Likert's writings is that the ideal and most productive leader behavior for industry is employee-centered or democratic. Yet his own findings raise questions as to whether there can be an ideal or single normatively good style of leader be-

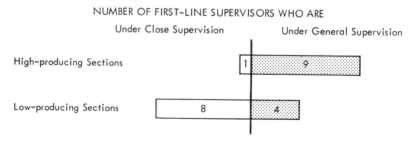

FIGURE 4.6 Low-production section heads are more closely supervised than high-production heads.

havior which can apply in all leadership situations. As the preceding figures revealed, one of the eight job-centered supervisors and one of the nine supervisors using close supervision had high-producing sections; also three of the nine employee-centered supervisors and four of the thirteen supervisors who used general supervision had low-producing sections. In other words, in almost 35 per cent of the low-producing sections, the suggested ideal type of leader behavior produced undesirable results and almost 15 per cent of the high-producing sections were supervised by the suggested "undesirable" style.

Further evidence suggesting that a single ideal or normative style of leader behavior is unrealistic was provided when a similar study was done in an industrial setting in Nigeria.[66] The results were almost the exact opposite to Likert's findings. In that country the tendency is for job-centered supervisors who provide close supervision to have high-producing sections, while the low-producing sections tend to have employee-centered supervisors who provide general supervision. Thus a single normative leadership style does not take into consideration cultural differences, particularly customs and traditions as well as the level of education and the standard of living. These are examples of cultural differences in the followers and the situation which are important in determining the appropriate leadership style to be used. Therefore, based on the definition of leadership process as a function of the leader, the followers, and other situational variables, the desire to have *a single ideal type of leader behavior seems unrealistic.*

ADAPTIVE LEADER BEHAVIOR

This desire to have an ideal type of leader behavior is common. Many managers appear to want to be told how to act. It is also clear from the preceding discussion that many writers in the field of leadership suggest some normative style. Most of these writers have supported either an integrated leadership style (high concern for both task and relationships) or a permissive, democratic, human relations approach. These styles might be appropriate in some industrial or educational settings in the United States, but they also may be limited to them. Effective leader behavior in other institutions such as the military, hospitals, prisons, churches, might very well be entirely different. Perhaps our formula should be modified to read: $E = f(l,f,s)$. The "E" stands for effectiveness. An effective leader is able to adapt his style of leader behavior to the needs of situation and the followers.

Since these are not constants, the use of an appropriate style of leader behavior is a challenge to the effective leader. "The manager must be much like the musician who changes his techniques and approaches to obtain the shadings of total performance desired." [67] The concept of *adaptive leader behavior* might be stated as follows:

> The more a manager adapts his style of leader behavior to meet the particular situation and the needs of his followers, the more effective he will tend to be in reaching personal and organizational goals.[68]

Leadership Contingency Model

The concept of adaptive leader behavior questions the existence of a "best" style of leadership: It is not a matter of the best style, but of the most effective style for a particular situation. The suggestion is that a number of leader behavior styles may be effective or ineffective depending on the important elements of the situation.

According to a Leadership Contingency Model developed by Fred E. Fiedler, there are three major situational variables which seem to determine whether a given situation is favorable or unfavorable to a leader: (1) His personal relations with the members of his group (leader-member relations); (2) The degree of structure in the task which the group has been assigned to perform (task structure); and (3) The power and authority which his position provides (position power).[69] Leader-member relations seems to parallel the relationships concepts discussed earlier, while task structure and position power, which measure very closely related aspects of a situation, seem to be related to task concepts. Fiedler defines the *favorableness of a situation* as "the degree to which the situation enables the leader to exert his influence over his group." [70]

In this model, there are eight possible combinations of these three situational variables that can occur. As a leadership situation varies from high to low on these variables, it will fall into one of the eight combinations (situations). The most favorable situation for a leader to influence his group is one in which he is well liked by the members (good leader-member relations), has a powerful position (high position power), and is directing a well-defined job (high task structure): for example, a well-liked general making inspection in an army camp. On the other hand, the most unfavorable situation is one in which the leader is disliked, has little position power, and faces an unstructured task: an unpopular chairman of a voluntary hospital fund-raising committee.

Having developed this model for classifying group situations, Fiedler has attempted to determine what the most effective leadership style—task-oriented or relationships-oriented—seems to be for each of the eight situations. In a re-examination of old leadership studies and analysis of new studies, in terms of his model, Fiedler has concluded that:

1. *Task-oriented* leaders tend to perform best in group situations which are either very favorable or very unfavorable to the leader.

2. *Relationships-oriented* leaders tend to perform best in situations which are intermediate in favorableness.[71]

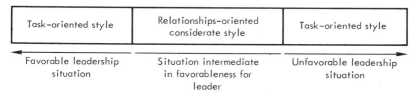

FIGURE 4.7 Leadership styles appropriate for various group situations.

While Fiedler's model is useful to a leader, he seems to be reverting to a single continuum of leader behavior, suggesting that there are only two basic leader behavior styles, task-oriented and relationships-oriented. It is felt that most evidence indicates that leader behavior must be plotted on two separate axes, rather than a single continuum. Thus a leader who has a high concern for tasks does not necessarily have a high or low concern for relationships. Any combination of the two dimensions may occur.

THE TRI-DIMENSIONAL LEADER EFFECTIVENESS MODEL

In the Tri-Dimensional Leader Effectiveness model which we will be discussing, the terms *task* and *relationships* will be used to describe the same concepts that the Ohio State Studies defined as *consideration* and *initiating structure*. For convenience sake, the four basic leader behavior quadrants will be labeled as high task, high task and relationships, high relationships, and low task and relationships as illustrated in Figure 4.8.

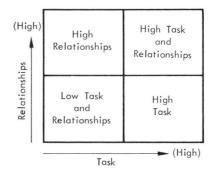

FIGURE 4.8 The basic leader behavior styles.

These four basic styles depict essentially leader personalities. As an individual matures he develops habit patterns or conditioned responses to various stimuli.

habit *a,* habit *b,* habit *c* . . . habit *n = personality*

An individual begins to behave in a similar fashion under similar conditions. This behavior is what others learn to recognize as that person, as his *personality.* They expect and can even predict certain kinds of behavior from him.

In the context of leader behavior, we are concerned about the portion of the total personality of an individual which we will call his *leader personality.* This is what some authors refer to as style. In the context of this book we will use the words "personality" and "style" interchangeably. The leader personality or style of an individual is the behavior pattern he exhibits when he is involved in directing the activities of others. The pattern generally involves either task-oriented behavior or relationships-oriented behavior or some combination of both. The two types of behavior, task-oriented and relationships-oriented, which are central to the concept of leader personality are defined as:

> *Task-Oriented Behavior*—The extent to which a leader is likely to organize and define the relationships between himself and the members of his group (followers); characterized by a tendency to define

the role which he expects each member of the group to assume, endeavoring to establish well-defined patterns of organization, channels of communication, and ways of getting jobs done.

Relationships-Oriented Behavior—The extent to which a leader is likely to maintain personal relationships between himself and the members of his group (followers); characterized by socio-emotional support such as friendship, mutual trust, respect for followers' ideas, consideration for their feelings.[72]

In brief, *task-oriented behavior* consists of structuring the relationships and activities in a group situation in terms of task accomplishment, while *relationships-oriented behavior* stresses building and maintaining good personal relations between himself and his followers.

There have been found leaders who are perceived by their followers, superiors, or associates as exhibiting one or more of the four basic leader personalities. These styles, derived from the task and relationships dimensions, can be described as follows:

High Task—With this leader personality, an individual is seen by others as high on task but low on relationships. He seems to be more concerned about the task at hand than he is about the personal feelings and satisfactions of his followers. He appears to emphasize the task aspects of productivity viewing members as tools to accomplish his own personal goals or the goals of his organization.

High Task and Relationships—With this leader personality, an individual is seen by others as high on both task and relationships. He appears to emphasize getting the task done, but not at the expense of the individuals in his group. He seems to set high standards but takes interest in everyone, accepting their individuality, personal needs, and ideas.

High Relationships—With this leader personality, an individual is seen by others as high on relationships but low on task. He appears to have a more overt concern for the needs of the individuals in the group than the task to be accomplished. He seems to feel that every individual is a human being and therefore treats everyone as if he were important. He tends to emphasize maximizing the support and development of his subordinates' potentials rather than maximizing productivity.

Low Task and Relationships—With this leader personality, an individual is seen by others as low on both task and relationships. He appears as a leader who allows his followers to direct their own activities and does not spend much time in developing personal relationships with them.

Effectiveness Dimension

Recognizing that the effectiveness of a leader depends on how his leader personality interrelates with the situation in which he operates, an effectiveness dimension should be added to the two dimensional model. This is illustrated in Figure 4.9.

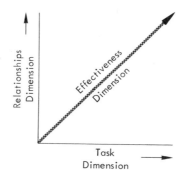

FIGURE 4.9   Adding an effectiveness dimension.

William J. Reddin in his 3-D Management Style Theory was the first to add an effectiveness dimension to the task and relationships dimensions of earlier models.[73] Reddin, whose pioneer work influenced greatly the development of the Tri-Dimensional Leader Effectiveness Model felt that a useful theoretical model "must allow that a variety of styles may be effective or ineffective depending on the situation." [74]

By adding an effectiveness dimension to the task and relationships dimensions of earlier leadership models, we are attempting to integrate the concepts of leader style with situational demands of a specific environment. When the style of a leader is appropriate to a given situation, it is termed *effective;* when his style is inappropriate to a given situation, it is termed *ineffective.*

If the effectiveness of a leader behavior style depends upon the situation in which it is used, it follows that any of the basic styles may be effective or ineffective depending on the situation. The difference between the effective and ineffective styles is often not the actual behavior of the leader, but the appropriateness of this behavior to the situation in which it is used. You might think of the leader's

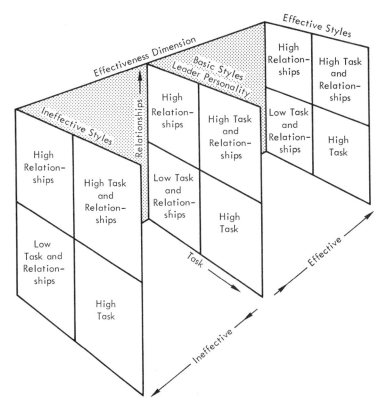

FIGURE 4.10   The Tri-Dimensional Leader
Effectiveness Model.

basic style as a particular stimulus, and it is the response to this
stimulus that can be considered effective or ineffective. This concept
is illustrated in the diagram of the Tri-Dimensional Leader Effectiveness Model presented in Figure 4.10.

The middle quadrants represent the four basic leader behavior
styles described and illustrated in Figure 4.8; the left quadrants illustrate the four basic styles when they are ineffective (used in an inappropriate situation); and the right quadrants illustrate the four basic
styles when they are effective (used in an appropriate situation).

The four effective and the four ineffective styles are, in essence,
how appropriate a leader's basic style is to a given situation as seen by
his followers, superiors or his associates. Table 4.1 describes briefly
how each style might be perceived by others.[75]

BASIC STYLES	EFFECTIVE	INEFFECTIVE
High Task	Often seen as knowing what he wants and imposing his methods for accomplishing this without creating resentment.	Often seen as having no confidence in others, unpleasant, and interested only in short-run output.
High Task and Relationships	Often seen as a good motivator who sets high standards, treats everyone differently, and prefers team management.	Often seen as a person who tries to please everyone and, therefore, vacillates back and forth to avoid pressures in a situation.
High Relationships	Often seen as having implicit trust in people and as being primarily concerned with developing their talents.	Often seen as primarily interested in harmony and being seen as "a good person," and being unwilling to risk disruption of a relationship to accomplish a task.
Low Task and Low Relationships	Often seen as appropriately permitting his subordinates to decide how the work should be done and playing only a minor part in their social interaction.	Often seen as uninvolved and passive, as a "paper shuffler," who cares little about the task at hand or the people involved.

TABLE 4.1.   How the basic leader behavior styles are
seen by others when they are effective or ineffective.

While effectiveness appears to be an either/or situation in this model, in reality, it should be represented as a continuum. Any given style in a particular situation could fall somewhere on this continuum from extremely effective to extremely ineffective. Effectiveness, therefore, is a matter of degree.

A model such as the Tri-Dimensional Leader Effectiveness Model is distinctive because it does not depict a single ideal leader behavior style which is suggested to be appropriate in all situations. For example, the high task and relationships style is appropriate only in certain situations. In basically crisis-oriented organizations like the military or the police, there is considerable evidence that the most appropriate style would be high task, since under combat or riot conditions success often depends upon immediate response to orders. Time demands do not permit talking things over or explaining decisions.

While a high task style might be effective for a combat officer, it may be ineffective in other situations even within the military. This was pointed out when line officers trained at West Point were sent to command outposts in the Dew Line which were part of an advanced warning system. The scientific personnel involved, living in close quarters in this Arctic region, did not respond favorably to the task-oriented behavior of those combat-trained officers. Their level of education and maturity was high and they did not need much structure in their work; in fact, they tended to resent it. In addition, many of these scientific and research people desired and needed few interpersonal relationships. In such situations, the low task and relationships style which has been assumed by some authors to be theoretically a poor leadership style may be the appropriate style to use.

Attitudinal vs. Behavioral Models

In examining the dimensions of the Managerial Grid (concern for production and concern for people), one can see that these are *attitudinal* dimensions. Concern is a feeling or emotion toward something. On the other hand, the dimensions of the Ohio State Model (initiating structure and consideration) and the Tri-Dimensional Leader Effectiveness Model (task behavior and relationships behavior) are dimensions of *observed* behavior. Thus, the Ohio State and Leader Effectiveness Models measure *how* people behave, while the Managerial Grid measures *predisposition* toward production and people.[76] As discussed earlier, the Tri-Dimensional Leader Effectiveness Model is an outgrowth of the Ohio State Model, but is distinctive because it adds an effectiveness dimension.

Although the Managerial Grid and the Leader Effectiveness Model measure different aspects of leadership, they are not incompatible. A conflict develops, however, because behavioral assumptions have often been drawn from analysis of the attitudinal dimensions of the Managerial Grid. While high *concern* for both production and people is desirable in organizations, managers having a high concern for both people and production do not always find it appropriate in all situations to initiate a high degree of structure and provide a high degree of socio-emotional support. For example, if a manager's subordinates are emotionally mature and can take responsibility for themselves, his appropriate style of leadership may be low task and low relationships. In this case, the manager permits these subordinates to participate in the planning, organizing and controlling of their own operation. He plays a background role, providing socio-emotional support only when necessary. Consequently, it is assumptions about behavior drawn from the Managerial Grid and not the Grid itself that are inconsistent with the Leader Effectiveness Model.

In summary, empirical studies tend to show that there is no normative (best) style of leadership; successful leaders can adapt their leader behavior to meet the needs of the group and of the particular situation. Effectiveness or productivity depends upon the leader, the followers, and other situational elements, $E = f(l,f,s)$. Therefore, those who are interested in increasing their own success as a leader must give serious thought to these behavioral and environmental considerations.

We have now discussed a number of approaches to the study of leader behavior, concluding with a Tri-Dimensional Leader Effectiveness Model. In Chapter Five we will discuss the effectiveness dimension in this model.

V

Determining
Effectiveness

The most important aspect of the Tri-Dimensional Leader Effectiveness Model is that it adds *effectiveness* to the task and relationships dimensions of earlier leadership models. For this reason, it seems appropriate to examine closely the concept of effectiveness.

MANAGEMENT EFFECTIVENESS VS. LEADERSHIP EFFECTIVENESS

In discussing effectiveness it is important to distinguish between management and leadership: management is working with and through people in an effort to accomplish organizational goals; leadership can occur in efforts to accomplish an individual's own goals. For example, a vice president may have a strong personal goal to become the company president. In attempting to achieve this goal, he may not be concerned with organizational goals at all, but only with undermining the plans of the president and other executives who might be contenders for the job. He may accomplish his goals, and, in that sense, be a successful leader. However, he could not be considered an effective manager, since his actions are probably disruptive to the effective operation of the firm. Thus, in discussing effectiveness we must recognize the difference between *individual goals, organizational goals, leadership,* and *management.*

POSITION POWER VS. PERSONAL POWER

Amitai Etzioni discusses the difference between *position power* and *personal power.* His distinction springs from his concept of power as the ability to induce or influence behavior. He claims that power is derived from an organizational office, personal influence, or both. An individual who is able to induce another individual to do a certain job because of his position in the organization is considered to have position power, while an individual who derives his power from his followers is considered to have personal power. Some individuals can have both position and personal power.[77]

SUCCESSFUL LEADERSHIP VS. EFFECTIVE LEADERSHIP

If an individual attempts to have some effect on the behavior of another, we call this attempted leadership. The response to this leadership attempt can be successful or unsuccessful. Since a manager's basic responsibility in any type of organization is to get work done with and through people, his success is measured by the output or productivity of the group he leads. With this thought in mind, we would like to make a clear distinction between *successful* and *effective* leadership or management.

Suppose manager A attempts to influence individual B to do a certain job. A's attempt will be considered successful or unsuccessful depending on the extent that B accomplishes the job. It is not really an either/or situation. A's success could be depicted on a continuum (Figure 5.1) ranging from very successful to very unsuccessful with gray areas in between which would be difficult to ascertain as either.

Let us assume that A's leadership is successful. In other words, B's response to A's leadership stimulus falls on the successful side of the continuum. This still does not tell the whole story of effectiveness.

If A's leader style is not compatible with the expectations of B and, if B is antagonized and does the job only because of A's position power, then we can say that A has been successful but not effective. B has responded as A intended because A has control of rewards and

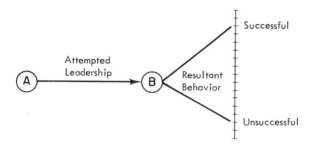

FIGURE 5.1   Successful-unsuccessful leadership continuum.

punishment, and not because B sees his own needs being accomplished by satisfying the goals of the manager or the organization.

On the other hand, if A's attempted leadership leads to a successful response, and B does the job because he wants to do it and finds it rewarding, then we consider A as having not only position power but also personal power. B respects A and is willing to cooperate with him, realizing that A's request is consistent with his own personal goals. In fact, B sees his own goals as being accomplished by this activity. This is what is meant by effective leadership, keeping in mind that effectiveness also appears as a continuum which can range from very effective to very ineffective as illustrated in Figure 5.2.

In the management of organizations, the difference between successful and effective often explains why many supervisors can get a satisfactory level of output only when they are right there, looking over the worker's shoulder. But as soon as they leave output declines and often such things as horseplay and scrap loss increase.

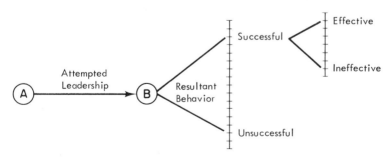

FIGURE 5.2   Successful and effective leadership
continuums.

The phenomenon described applies not only to business organizations but also to less formal organizations like the family. If parents are successful and effective, have both position and personal power, their children accept family goals as their own. Consequently, if the husband and wife leave for the weekend, the children behave no differently than if their parents were there. If, on the other hand, the parents continually use close supervision and the children view their own goals as being stifled by their parents goals, the parents have only position power. They maintain order because of the rewards and punishments they control. If these parents went away on a trip leaving the children behind, upon returning they might be greeted by havoc and chaos.

In summary, a manager could be successful, but ineffective, having only short-run influence over the behavior of others. On the other hand, if a manager is both successful and effective, his influence tends to lead to long-run productivity and organizational development.

WHAT DETERMINES ORGANIZATIONAL EFFECTIVENESS?

In discussing effectiveness we have concentrated on evaluating the results of individual leaders or managers. While these results are significant, perhaps the most important aspect of effectiveness is its relationship to an entire organization. Here we are concerned not only about the outcome of a given leadership attempt, but with the effectiveness of the organizational unit over a period of time.

In evaluating effectiveness, perhaps more than ninety per cent of managers in organizations look at measures of output alone. Thus, the effectiveness of a business manager is often determined by net profits, the effectiveness of a college professor may be determined by the number of articles and books he has published, and the effectiveness of a basketball coach may be determined by his won-lost record.

Many researchers too talk about effectiveness emphasizing output variables. Fred E. Fiedler, for example, in his studies evaluated "leader effectiveness in terms of group performance on the group's primary assigned task." [78] William J. Reddin, in discussing management styles, thinks in similar terms about effectiveness. He argues that the effectiveness of a manager should be measured "objectively by his profit center performance"—maximum output, market share, or other similar criteria. [79]

Others feel that it is unrealistic to think only in terms of productivity or output in evaluating organizational effectiveness. According to Rensis Likert, another class of variables that "reflect the current condition of the internal state of the organization: its loyalty, skills, motivations, and capacity for effective interaction, communication, and decision-making are too often neglected in evaluations of managers." [80] He calls these variables *intervening variables*. In essence, intervening variables are concerned with building and developing the organization, and tend to be long-term goals. Managers are often promoted, however, on the basis of short-run output variables such as increased production and earnings, without concern for the long-run and organizational development. This creates a dilemma.

Organizational Dilemma

One of the major problems in industry today is that there is a shortage of successful managers. Therefore, it is not uncommon for a manager to be promoted in six months or a year if he is a "producer." Since the basis on which top management promotes is often short-run output, managers attempt to achieve high levels of productivity, and often overemphasize tasks, placing extreme pressure on everyone, even when it is inappropriate.

We have all probably had some experience with coming into an office or home and raising the roof with subordinates. The immediate or short-run effect is probably increased productivity. We also know that if this style is inappropriate for those concerned, and if it continues over a long period of time, the morale and climate of the organization will deteriorate. Some indications of deterioration of these intervening variables at work may be turnover, absenteeism, increased accidents, scrap loss, and numerous grievances. Not only the number of grievances, but the nature of grievances is important. Are grievances really significant problems or do they reflect pent up emotions due to anxieties and frustration? Are they settled at the complaint stage between the employee and supervisor or are they pushed up the hierarchy to be settled at higher levels or by arbitration? The organizational dilemma is that in many instances, a manager who places pressure on everyone and produces in the short run, is promoted out of this situation before the disruptive aspects of the intervening variables catch up.

There tends to be a time lag between declining intervening variables and significant restriction of output by employees under such management climate. Employees tend to feel "things will get better."

Thus, when the manager is promoted rapidly, he often stays "one step ahead of the wolf."

The real problem is faced by the next manager. Although productivity records are high, he has inherited many problems. Merely the introduction of a new manager may be enough to collapse the slowly deteriorating intervening variables. A tremendous drop in morale and motivation leading almost immediately to significant decrease in output can occur. Change by its very nature is frightening; to a group whose intervening variables are declining, it can be devastating. Regardless of this new manager's style, the present expectations of the followers may be so distorted, that much time and patience will be needed to close the now apparent "credibility gap" between the goals of the organization and the personal goals of the group. No matter how effective this manager might be in the long run, his superiors in reviewing a productivity drop, may give him only a few months to improve performance. But as Likert's studies indicate, rebuilding a group's intervening variables in a small organization may take one to three years, and in a large organization, it may extend to seven years. This dilemma is not restricted to business organizations.

In one of Fiedler's studies he examined the leadership in basketball teams. The criterion he used in evaluating the effectiveness of these leaders was percentage of games—won and lost. Most people also tend to evaluate coaches on won and lost records.

Charlie, a high school coach, has had several good seasons. He knows if he has one more such season he will have a job offer with a better salary at a more prestigious school. Under these conditions, he may decide to concentrate on the short-run potential of the team. He may play only his seniors and he may have an impressive record at the end of the season. Short-run output goals have been maximized, but the intervening variables of the team have been drained. If Charlie leaves this school and accepts another job, a new coach will find himself with a tremendous rebuilding job. But because developing the freshmen and sophomores and rebuilding a good team takes time and much work, the team could have a few poor seasons in the interim. When the alumni and fans see the team losing, they soon forget that old adage, "It's not whether you win or lose, it's how you play the game." They immediately consider the new coach "a bum." After all, "We had some great seasons with good ole Charlie." It is difficult for them to realize that the previous coach concentrated only on short-run winning at the expense of building for the future. The problem is that the effectiveness of a new coach is judged immediately on the same games won basis as his predecessor. He may be doing an excellent job of rebuilding and might have a winning season in two or three years, but the probability of his being given the opportunity to build a future winner is low.

It should be clear that we do not think this is an either/or process. It is often a matter of determining how much to concentrate on each. In our basketball example, suppose a team has good potential, having a large number of experienced senior players, but as the season progresses it does not look like it is going to be an extremely good year. There comes a point in this season when the coach must make a basic decision. Will he continue to play his experienced seniors and hope to win a majority of his final games, or should he forget about concentrating on winning the last games and play his sophomores and juniors to give them experience, in hopes of developing and building a winning team for future years? The choice is between short- and long-term goals. If the accepted goal is building and developing the team for the future, then the coach should be evaluated on these terms and not entirely on his present won-lost record.

While intervening variables do not appear on won-lost records, balance sheets, sales reports, or accounting ledgers, we feel that these long-term considerations are just as important to an organization as short-term output variables. Therefore, although difficult to measure, intervening variables should not be overlooked in determining organizational effectiveness. One of the instruments used by Likert to measure these variables was discussed in Chapter Three.

In summary, we feel that effectiveness is actually determined by whatever the manager and the organization decide are their goals and objectives, but should consider both output and intervening variables, and short and long-range goals. Managers in these organizations should also be judged in these terms.

PARTICIPATION AND EFFECTIVENESS

In an organizational setting, it is urged that the criteria for an individual or a group's performance should be mutually decided in advance. In making these decisions, a manager and his subordinates should consider output and intervening variables, short- and long-range goals. This process has two advantages. First, it will permit subordinates to participate in determining the basis on which their efforts will be judged. Second, involving subordinates in the planning process will increase their commitment to the goals and objectives established. Research evidence seems to support this contention.

One of the classic studies in this area was done by Coch and French in an American factory.[81] They found that when managers and employees discussed proposed technological changes productivity increased and resistance to change decreased once these procedures were initiated. Other studies[82] have shown similar results. These studies suggest that involving employees in decision-making tends to be effective in our society. Once again, though, we must remember that the success of using participative management depends on the situation. While this approach tends to be effective in some industrial settings in America, it may not be appropriate in other countries.

This argument was illustrated clearly when French, Israel and Ås attempted to replicate the original Coch and French experiment in a Norwegian factory.[83] In this setting, they found no significant difference in productivity between work groups in which participative management was used and those in which it was *not* used. In other words, increased participation in decision-making did not have the same positive influence on factory workers in Norway as it did in America. Similar to Hersey's replication of one of Likert's studies in Nigeria, this Norwegian study suggests that cultural differences in the followers and the situation may be important in determining the appropriate leadership style.

STYLE AND EFFECTIVENESS

Examples of additional research which support the argument that all the basic leader behavior styles may be effective or ineffective depending on the situation are readily available.

A. K. Korman[84] gathered some of the most convincing evidence which dispels the idea of a single best style of leader behavior. Korman attempted to review all studies which examined the relationships between the Ohio State behavior dimensions of initiating structure (task) and consideration (relationships) and various measures of effectiveness, including group productivity, salary, performance under stress, administrative reputation, work group grievances, absenteeism, and turnover. In all, over twenty-five studies were reviewed. In every case the two dimensions were measured by either the Leadership Opinion Questionnaire or the Leader Behavior Description Questionnaire. The former is used to assess how a leader thinks he should behave in a given situation, while the latter measures follower perceptions of leader behavior. Korman concluded that:

Despite the fact that "Consideration" and "Initiating Structure" have become almost bywords in American industrial psychology, it seems apparent that very little is now known as to how these variables may predict work group performance and the conditions which affect such predictions. At the current time, we cannot even say whether they have any predictive significance at all.[85]

Thus, Korman found consideration and initiating structure had no significant predictive value in terms of effectiveness. This suggests that since situations differ, so must leader style.

Fred Fiedler, in testing his contingency model of leadership in over fifty studies covering a span of sixteen years (1951–67), concluded that both directive, task-oriented leaders and non-directive, human relations-oriented leaders are successful under some conditions. As Fiedler argues:

While one can never say that something is impossible, and while someone may well discover the all-purpose leadership style or behavior at some future time, our own data and those which have come out of sound research by other investigators do not promise such miraculous cures.[86]

A number of other investigators [87] besides Likert, Korman, and Fiedler have also shown that *different leadership situations require different leader styles*. In summary, the evidence is clear that there is no single, all-purpose leader behavior style that is effective in all situations.

THE MODEL AND OTHER RESEARCH

By using the Tri-Dimensional Leader Effectiveness Model, we can better understand occurrences in other research such as the unexplained cases in Likert's studies. As you will recall, in one study Likert found that six of seven high-producing sections had employee-centered supervisors, while seven of ten low-producing sections had job-centered supervisors. In organizing the findings, Likert only reported that employee-centered supervisors tended to be higher producers than job-centered supervisors. He did not discuss the one high-producing job-centered supervisor and the three low-producing employee-centered supervisors. With the Tri-Dimensional Leader Effectiveness model, not only can we account for the effectiveness of employee-centered (high relationships) leader behavior in certain situations, but we can also discuss its ineffectiveness in other situations. The same can be done with job-centered (high task) leader behavior. The findings from Likert's study could thus be illustrated in our model as follows.

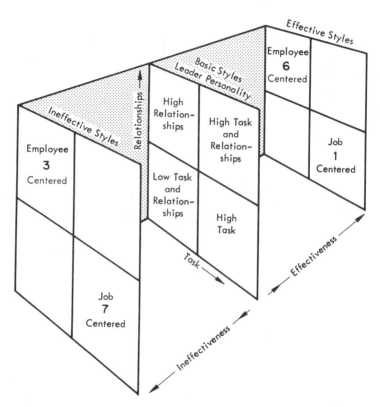

FIGURE 5.3 A Likert study and the Tri-Dimensional Leader Effectiveness Model.

Figure 5.3 seems to suggest that Likert recognizes only two leader behavior styles—high relationships and high task. This interpretation might be unfair to Likert because his definition of employee-centered supervisors tends to imply that a high relationships-oriented leader might also be somewhat high on task, thus including both the high relationships and high tasks and relationships styles of our model.

As discussed earlier William J. Reddin has developed a similar model depicting an effectiveness dimension.[88] Giving popular labels to both effective and ineffective managerial styles, Reddin has been using this model in management development programs in Canada and other countries. One of the main differences between the two models is that Reddin is concerned only with management styles while we are concerned also with leadership styles.

The distinction between management and leadership is important. Reddin defines a manager as, "A person occupying a position in a formal organization who is responsible for the work of at least one other person and who has formal authority over that person." [89] This definition is consistent with our contention that management is working with and through people in an effort to accomplish organizational goals. Thus when Reddin talks about management styles he is limiting his discussion to a formal organizational setting. Leadership, as we defined it, can occur in efforts to accomplish organizational goals, but it may also appear in efforts to accomplish merely individual goals, i.e., obtaining power or controlling the rate of production. In fact, as the Hawthorne studies revealed, the informal leadership which develops in any organization can be a powerful element affecting productivity. Consequently, the Tri-Dimensional Leader Effectiveness Model applies to more situations than a model which is limited only to formal organizational settings.

ENVIRONMENTAL VARIABLES

In managing for organizational effectiveness, a manager must first be able to diagnose his own leader behavior (personality) in light of his environment. Other variables which he should examine include the organization, superiors, associates, followers, and job demands.[90] This list is not all-inclusive, but contains some of the interacting components that tend to be important to a manager as illustrated in Figure 5.4, page 92.

While our basic conclusion in this chapter is that the type of leader behavior needed depends on the situation, this conclusion leaves many questions unanswered for a specific individual in a leadership role. Such an individual may be personally interested in how leadership depends on the situation and how he can find some practical value in theory. To accommodate this type of concern, in Chapter Six, we will discuss applications of the Tri-Dimensional Effectiveness Model. In this discussion an attempt will be made to provide the individual with a framework which will help him make effective decisions in problematic leadership situations.

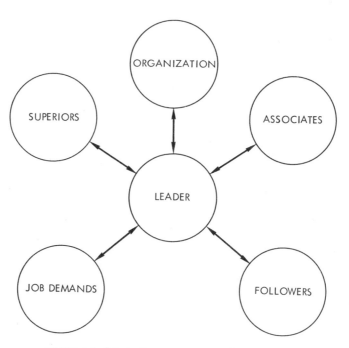

FIGURE 5.4 Interacting components of an organizational setting.

VI

Managing for Organizational Effectiveness

The Tri-Dimensional Leader Effectiveness Model is built on the concept that effectiveness results from a leader using a behavior style which is appropriate to the demands of the environment. This environment consists of the leader, followers, and the other situational elements of the organization. Therefore, an effective leader must be able to *diagnose* the demands of the environment, and then either *adapt* his leader personality to fit these demands, or develop the means to *change* some or all of the other variables.

LEADER AND ENVIRONMENT

As we discussed in the last chapter, there are a number of interacting components of a leader's environment. The leader must learn to analyze these components accurately. Some of the environmental variables he must be able to appraise are:

Leader's personality
Leader's expectations
Followers' personalities

Followers' expectations
Superiors' personalities
Superior's expectations
Associates' personalities
Associates' expectations
Organization's personality
Organization's expectations
Job Demands

Personality Defined

As previously discussed, we are using the terms *personality* and *style* interchangeably. Personality is defined as consistent behavior patterns of an individual as perceived by others. These patterns emerge as an individual begins to respond in the same fashion under similar conditions; he develops habits of action which become somewhat predictable to those who work with him.

Expectations Defined

Expectations are the perceptions of appropriate behavior for one's own role or position or one's perceptions of the roles of others within the organization. In other words, the expectations of an individual define for him what he should do under various circumstances in his particular job and how he thinks others—his superiors, peers, and subordinates—should behave in relation to his position. To say that a person has *shared expectations* with another person means that each of the individuals involved perceives accurately and accepts his role and the role of the other. If expectations are to be compatible it is important to share common goals and objectives. While two people might have differing personalities because their roles require different styles of behavior, it is imperative for an organization's effectiveness that they perceive and accept the institution's goals and objectives as their own.

PERSONALITY AND EXPECTATIONS

Behavior of an individual in an organizational setting results from the interaction of personality and expectations. Some positions are structured greatly by expectations; that is, they allow the person occupying that position very little room to express his individual personality. The behavior of an army private, for example, may be said to conform almost completely to role expectations.[91] Little innovative behavior is tolerated. In highly structured, routine jobs based on Theory X assumptions about human nature, the behavior required by an individual is predetermined.

On the other hand, some positions have fewer formal expectations, allowing for more individual latitude in expressing one's personality. The behavior of a research chemist, for example, is derived extensively from his personality and innovation and creativity are encouraged. It seems that as an individual moves to a more responsible job, personality becomes more important and expectations become less structured.

While the mix varies from job to job, behavior in an organization remains a function of both personality and expectations and involves some combination of task and relationships orientation.

Leader's Personality and Expectations

One of the most important elements of a leadership situation is the personality of the leader himself. The leader develops this *style* over a period of time from experience, education, and training. This style is not how the leader thinks he behaves in his situation but how others (most importantly, his followers) perceive his behavior. This is often a difficult concept for a leader to understand. If a leader's followers think he is a hard-nosed task-oriented leader, this is very valuable information for him to know. In fact, it makes little difference whether he thinks he is a relationships-oriented, democratic leader, because his followers will behave according to how *they* perceive his behavior. In this case, the followers will treat the leader as if he were a hard-nosed, task-oriented leader. Thus, a leader has to learn how he is coming across to others. Yet this kind of information is difficult to obtain. People are often reluctant to be honest with one another on this subject, especially if they are in a superior-subordinate relationship.

One method which has been developed to help individuals learn how others perceive their behavior is "sensitivity or T-group training." This method of training was developed at Bethel, Maine, in 1947, by Leland P. Bradford, Kenneth D. Benne, and Gordon Lippitt.[92] It is based on the assumption that a number of individuals meeting in an unstructured situation with an open climate will develop working relations with each other and learn a great deal about themselves as perceived by the other group members.

The training process relies primarily and almost exclusively on the behavior experienced by the participants; i.e., the *group itself* becomes the focus of inquiry . . . In short, the participants learn to analyze and become more sensitive to the processes of human interaction and acquire concepts to order and control these phenomena.[93]

An example follows of one of Chris Argyris' experiences with a T-group where the president and nine vice presidents of a large industrial organization went into a retreat for a week to discuss their problems.

At the outset, after defining the objectives of this educational experience, the seminar leader said, in effect, "O.K. Let's go." There was a very loud silence and someone said, "What do you want us to do?"

(Silence.)

"Where's the agenda?"

(Silence.)

"Look, here, what's going on? Aren't you going to lead this?"

(Silence.)

"I didn't come up here to feel my stomach move. What's up?"

(Silence.)

"Fellows, if he doesn't speak in five minutes, I'm getting out of here."

"Gentlemen," said the treasurer, "We've paid for the day, so let's remain at least till five."

"You know, there's something funny going on here."

"What's funny about it?"

"Well, up until a few minutes ago we trusted this man enough that all of us were willing to leave the company for a week. Now we dislike him. Why? He hasn't done anything."

"That's right. And it's his job to do something. He's the leader and he ought to lead."

"But I'm learning something already about how we react under these conditions. I honestly feel uncomfortable and somewhat fearful. Does anybody else?"

"That's interesting that you mention fear, because I think that we run the company by fear."

The president turned slightly red and became annoyed: "I don't think that we run this company by fear and I don't think you should have said that."

A loud silence followed. The vice president thought for a moment, took a breath, looked the president straight in the eye and said, "I still think we run this company by fear and I agree with you. I should not have said it."

The group laughed and the tension was broken.

"I'm sorry," the president said. "I wanted all you fellows with me here so that we can try to develop a higher sense of openness and trust. The first one that really levels with us, I let him have it. I'm sorry—but it isn't easy to hear about management by fear . . ."

"And it's not easy to tell you."

"Why not? Haven't I told you that my door is open?"

And the group plunged into the issue of how they judge the openness of a person—by the way he speaks or by the way he behaves? [94]

Argyris reported that:

The group explored their views about each other—the way each individual tended unintentionally to inhibit the other (the vice presidents learned that they inhibited each other as much as the president did, but for years had felt it was his fault); their levels of aspiration, their goals in their company life and in their total life; their ways of getting around each other, ranging from not being honest with one another to creating organizational fires which had to be put out by someone else; their skill at polarizing issues when deep disagreements occurred so that the decisions could be bucked right up to the president, who would have to take the responsibility and the blame; their techniques in the game of one-upmanship, etc.[95]

The result was highly satisfying. Once these top executives returned home, they found that they could reduce the number of meetings, the time spent at meetings, the defensive politicking, and the wind-milling at the lower levels. In time they also found that they could truly delegate more responsibility, get more valid information up from the ranks, and make the decisions more freely.

Although the main objective of T-group Training was originally personal growth or self-insight, the process is now being used extensively to implement organization improvement or change.[96] It should be remembered, though, that this approach is relatively new and still being developed. It has some critics as well as advocates among organizations which have experimented with these techniques.

All leaders have expectations about the way they should behave in a certain situation. How they actually behave often depends on these expectations. The resulting behavior, though is sometimes modified by the impact of how they interpret the expectations of other persons in their environment, i.e., how they feel their boss expects them to operate.

Followers' Personalities and Expectations

The personalities or styles of his followers (subordinates) is an important consideration for a leader in appraising his situation. In fact, as Fillmore Sanford has indicated, there is some justification for regarding the followers "as the most crucial factor in any leadership event." [97] Followers in any situation are vital, not only because individually they accept or reject the leader, but as a group they actually determine whatever personal power he may have.

This element is important at all levels of management. Victor H. Vroom has uncovered evidence that the effectiveness of a leader is dependent to a great extent on the personality or style of the individual workers.[98]

> Place a group with strong independence drives under a supervisor who needs to keep his men under his thumb, and the result is very likely to be trouble. Similarly, if you take docile men who are accustomed to obedience and respect for their supervisors and place them under a supervisor who tries to make them manage their own work, they are likely to wonder uneasily whether he really knows what he is doing.[99]

Therefore, even though a manager would prefer to change his followers' styles, he may find that he must adapt, at least temporarily, to their present behavior. For example, a supervisor who wants his subordinates to take more responsibility and to operate under general rather than close supervision, cannot expect this kind of change to take place overnight. His current behavior, at least to some extent, must be compatible to the present expectations of the group with planned change taking place over a long term period.

A leader should know the expectations followers have about the way he should behave in certain situations. This is especially important if a leader is new in his position. His predecessor's leader behavior style is then a powerful influence. If this style is different from the one the leader plans to use, this may create an immediate problem.[100] The leader must either change his style to coincide with followers' expectations or change their expectations. Since the leader's style has often been developed over a long period of time, it can be difficult for him to make any drastic changes in the short run. It might, therefore, be more effective if he concentrates on changing the expectations of his followers. In other words, in some cases he may be able to convince his followers that his style, while not what they normally would expect, if accepted, will be adequate.

Superiors' Personalities and Expectations

Another element of the environment is the leader personality of one's boss. Everyone has a boss of one kind or another. While most managers give considerable attention to supervising subordinates, some do not pay enough attention to being a subordinate themselves, and yet meeting the superior's expectations is often an important factor affecting one's style. If your boss is very task-oriented, for example, he might expect his subordinate to operate in the same manner. Relationships-oriented behavior might be evaluated as inappropriate, without even considering results. This has become evident when first-line supervisors are sent to training programs to improve their "human relations skills." Upon returning to the plant, they try to implement some of these new ideas in working with their people. Yet, because their superior has not accepted these concepts, he becomes impatient with the first-line supervisor's new-found concern for people. "Joe, cut out all that talking with the men and get the work out." With such reactions, it would not take the supervisor long to revert to his old style, and in the future, it will be much more difficult to implement any change in his behavior.

It is important for a manager to know his boss's expectations, particularly if he wants to advance in the organization. If he is predisposed toward promotion, he may tend to adhere to the customs and mores (styles and expectations) of the group to which he aspires to join, rather than his peer group.[101] Consequently, his superiors' expectations have become more important to him than other groups with which he interacts—his followers or associates.

Associates' Personalities and Expectations

A leader's associates or peers are those individuals who have similar positions within the organization. For example, the associates of a vice president for production are the other vice presidents in his company.

The styles and expectations of one's associates are important when a leader has frequent interaction with them, for example, a situation which involves trading and bargaining for resources, such as budget money.[102]

In discussing superiors we mentioned the manager who has a strong drive to advance in an organization. Some people, however, are satisfied with their present position. For these people, the expectations of their associates may be more important in influencing their behavior than those of their superiors. College professors tend to be good examples. Often they are more concerned about their peer group, other professors or colleagues in their area of expertise, than they are in being promoted to administrative positions. As a result, college presidents and deans often have little position power with professors.

Organization's Personality and Expectations

The personality and expectations of an organization are determined by the history and tradition of the organization as well as by the organizational goals and objectives which reflect the style and expectations of present top management.

Over a period of time, an organization, much like an individual, becomes characterized by certain modes of behavior which are perceived as *its* personality or style. The development of an organizational personality or "corporate image" has been referred to as the process of institutionalization.[103] In this process, the organization is infused with a system of values that reflect its history and the people who have played vital roles in its formation and growth. Thus, it is difficult to understand Ford Motor Company without knowing the impact which Henry Ford had on its formation.

Members of the organization soon become conscious of the value system operating within the institution and guide their actions from many expectations derived from these values. The organization's expectations are most often expressed in forms of policy, operating procedures and controls, as well as in informal customs and mores developed over time.

Organizational Goals

The goals of an organization usually consist of some combination of output and intervening variables. As we have discussed earlier, output variables are those short-run goals which can be easily measured, such as net profits, annual earnings, won-lost record, etc. On the other hand, intervening variables consist of those long-run goals reflecting the internal condition of the organization which can *not* easily be measured, such as its capacity for effective interaction, communication, and decision-making. These organizational goals can be expressed in terms of task and relationships as illustrated in Figure 6.1.

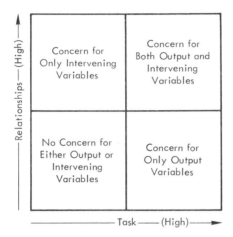

FIGURE 6.1 Organizational goals as expressed in terms of task and relationships.

OTHER SITUATIONAL VARIABLES

Job Demands

Another important element of a leadership situation is the demands of the job that the leader's group has been assigned to perform. Fiedler [104] called this situational variable *task structure.* He found that a task which has specific instructions on what the leader and his followers should do requires a different leadership style than an unstructured task that has no prescribed operating procedures. Research findings indicate that highly *structured* jobs which need directions seem to require high task behavior, while *unstructured* jobs which do not need directions seem to favor relationships-oriented behavior.

The *amount of interaction* the job requires of subordinates is another important consideration for a manager in analyzing his work environment. Vroom and Floyd H. Mann studied this aspect of a job in a large trucking company.[105] They investigated two groups of workers: One group was involved in the package and handling operation and the other consisted of truck drivers and their dispatchers. The nature of the work in the package and handling operation required that the men work closely together in small groups. Cooperation and teamwork was required, not only among the workers, but between the workers and their superiors. In this situation, the workers preferred and worked better under employee-centered supervisors. The truck drivers, on the other hand, usually worked alone, having little contact with other people. These men did not depend on others for accomplishing their task. The only exceptions were the dispatchers from whom they needed accurate information. Since the truck drivers generally worked alone, they were not concerned about harmony, but were concerned about the structure of the job in terms of where and when they were to deliver or pick up. In this situation, they preferred task-oriented supervisors.

Time

There are other important elements in the environment of a leader which we have not discussed. One variable which needs to be mentioned, though, is the *time duration available for decision-making*. If a manager's work area burst into flames, he could not seek opinions and suggestions from his followers or use other methods of involvement to obtain the best way to leave the building. The leader must make an immediate decision and point the way. Therefore, short time demands, such as in an emergency, tend to require task-oriented behavior. On the other hand, if time is not a major factor in the situation, there is more opportunity to use other styles of leadership.

STYLE ADAPTABILITY

Adaptability is the range of behavior within which a leader can vary his style. If the variation is appropriate to the situation, the leader will be effective, if it is inappropriate, the leader tends to be ineffective.

Leaders differ in their ability to vary their style to different situations. Some leaders are able to modify their behavior to fit any of the four basic styles, while others can utilize two or three styles. Adaptive leaders have the potential to be effective in a number of situations. (This flexibility alone is not the key to effectiveness; it is essential that the leader change his style appropriately.) Other leaders seem to be limited to one basic style. As a result, rigid leaders tend to be effective only in situations where their styles are compatible with the environment.

Low and High Adaptability Demands

Leadership situations vary in the extent to which they make demands on adaptability. William J. Reddin has cited some of the conditions which demand, in his terms, low and high flexibility. These conditions are listed below in Table 6.1.

Low Flexibility Demands	*High Flexibility Demands*
Low-level managerial jobs	High-level managerial jobs
Simple managerial jobs	Complex managerial jobs
Established goals	Emerging goals
Tight procedures	Fluid procedures
Established tasks	Unstructured tasks
Routine, automated, decision-making	Nonroutine decision-making
Little environmental change	Rapid environmental change
Manager has complete power	Manager does not have complete power
Following plans essential	Using initiative essential
Manager accepted or rejected by sub-ordinates	Subordinates neutral to manager
Few interconnecting jobs	Many interconnecting jobs

TABLE 6.1 Low and high flexibility demands.[106]

Some jobs require a high degree of adaptability, other jobs have low demands on adaptability.

High Adaptability Job

The president of a college or university must continually deal with numerous groups, including his board of trustees, administrative staff, faculty, and students. With his board of trustees, he might have to "talk softly but carry a big stick"; with his administrative staff, he might have to be task-oriented, and stress planning, organizing, and controlling; with his faculty, he might have to act like a salesman and push for his ideas; with his student body, he may want to appear relationships-oriented, emphasizing morale and school spirit; while with an individual problem student, he may want to take a firm stand. In dealing with each of these groups, a different leadership style might be appropriate.

Low Adaptability Job

A sergeant supervising a large group of draftees in an army boot camp might be able to use the same style with all his men. He may act toward everyone in a cold manner. Since he is training these men for possible battle, he must emphasize and demand strict discipline. Therefore, he might effectively be task-oriented in almost everything he does.

Determining Style Range

The style range of a leader can be illustrated in terms of task and relationships [107] as shown in Figure 6.2. The shape of the circle indicates the range of style. If the shape has a small area as in A, then the range of behavior of the leader is limited; whereas if it has a large area, as in B, the leader has a wide range of behavior.

In A, the leader has basically a relationships-oriented style with little flexibility; in B, however, the leader has a broad range of leader behavior, and is able to use, to some extent, any of the four basic styles. In this example, A may be effective in situations which demand a re-

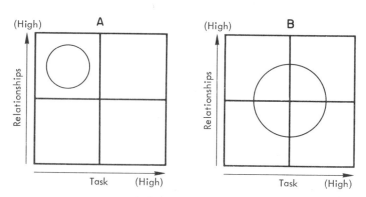

FIGURE 6.2   Style range in terms of task and relationships.

lationships-oriented style, i.e., in coaching or counseling situations. B, however, has the potential to be effective in a wide variety of instances. It should be remembered, though, that his style flexibility will not guarantee effectiveness. B will be effective only if he changes his style appropriately to fit the situation. This fact emphasizes the importance of a leader's *diagnostic* ability: [108] His ability to understand the nature and impact of the environmental variables discussed earlier and to evaluate them in terms of task and relationship demands.

DIAGNOSING THE TOTAL ENVIRONMENT

Any of the situational elements we have discussed may be analyzed in terms of task and relationships. Let us take the case of Steve, a general foreman who has been offered a promotion to superintendent in another plant. In his present position, which he has held for fifteen years, Steve has been extremely effective as a task-oriented manager responsible for the operation of several assembly-line processes.

The first impulse is for Steve to immediately accept this promotion in status and salary and move his family to the new location. But instead, he feels it is important first to visit the plant and to talk with some of the people with whom he will be working. In talking with these people, Steve may gain some insight into some of the important dimensions of this new position. An analysis of all these variables in terms of task and relationships could be summarized together as illustrated [109] in Figure 6.3. If Steve, using diagnostic skills, makes this type of analysis, he has gone a long way toward gathering

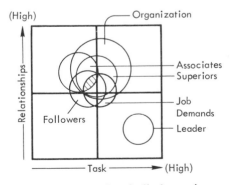

FIGURE 6.3 An example of all the environmental variables being analyzed together in terms of task and relationships.

the necessary information he needs for effectively determining his appropriate actions.

Each of the circles represents the combined style and expectations of one of the environmental variables. The shaded area indicates where the demands of these variables intersect. If Steve took the superintendent's job, he would probably have to operate within this area to maximize his effectiveness. In this plant, the situation seems to demand a moderately high task and relationships-oriented superintendent. Unfortunately though, Steve's style and expectations do not intersect any of the other variables, and his personality tends to be limited to task-oriented behavior. Thus, if he accepts the job and makes no changes, there is a high probability that Steve will be ineffective. At this point, he has to make a decision. Several other alternatives are available to him.

1. He can attempt to expand his range of behavior, thus bringing himself into the area of effectiveness.

2. He can attempt to change some or all of the situational elements. For example, he can attempt to change the behavior and the expectations of his followers through training and development programs and/or coaching and counseling.

3. He can attempt to make *some* changes in both his own range of behavior and some or all of the situational elements, thus attempting in the long-run to have the two move toward each other, rather than concentrating only on changing one or the other.

4. He can reject the job and seek another superintendent's position in an environment where his range of behavior is more compatible to the demands of the other situational elements.

5. He can remain in his present position where he knows he has been effective and will probably continue to be.

While this example has been written from the point of view of an individual, this type of analysis is just as important from an organization's point of view. It is vital that the men placed in key positions throughout the organization have the prerequisites for carrying out the organizational goals effectively. Management must realize that it does not follow that a man will be effective in one position merely because he has been effective in another situation.

Although Steve's is a special case, the alternatives available to him are similar to those faced by many leaders. Let us examine some of the factors involved in these alternatives in more detail.

Changing Style

One of the most difficult changes to make is a complete change in the personality of a person, and yet industry invests many millions of dollars annually for training and development programs which concentrate on changing the style of its leaders. As Fiedler suggests:

> A person's leadership style reflects the individual's basic motivational and need structure. At best it takes one, two, or three years of intensive psychotherapy to effect lasting changes in personality structure. It is difficult to see how we can change in more than a few cases an equally important set of core values in a few hours of lectures and role playing or even in the course of a more intensive training program of one or two weeks.[110]

Fiedler's point is well-taken. It is indeed difficult to effect changes in the styles of managers overnight. However, it is not completely hopeless. But, at best, it is a slow and expensive process that requires creative planning and patience. In fact, Likert found that it takes from three to seven years, depending on the size and complexity of the organization, to effectively implement a new management theory.

> Haste is self-defeating because of the anxieties and stresses it creates. There is no substitute for ample time to enable the members of an organization to reach the level of skillful and easy, habitual use of the new leadership.[111]

What generally happens in present training and development programs is that managers are encouraged to adopt certain normative behavior styles. In our culture, these styles are usually high relationships or high task and relationships styles. While we agree that there is a growing tendency for these two styles to be more effective than the high task or low task and relationships styles, we recognize that this is not universally the case, even in our own culture. In fact, it is often not the case, even within a single work group. While most workers might respond favorably to the high relationships-oriented styles, a few might react to these styles in a negative manner, taking advantage of what they consider a "soft touch." As a result, certain individuals will have to be handled in a different way. Perhaps, they will only respond to the proverbial "kick in the pants" (a high task-oriented style). Thus, it is unrealistic to think that any of these styles can be successfully applied everywhere. In addition to considering application, it is questionable whether every leader can adapt to one "normative" style.

Most training and development programs do not recognize these two considerations. Consequently, a foreman who has been operating as a task-oriented, authoritarian leader for many years is encouraged to change his style—"get in step with the times." Upon returning from the training program, the foreman will probably try to utilize some of the new relationships-oriented techniques he has recently been taught. The problem is that his personality is not compatible with the new concepts. As long as things are running smoothly, he has no difficulty using them. However, the minute an important issue or crisis develops he tends to revert back to his old basic style and becomes inconsistent, vacillating between the new relationships-oriented style he has been taught, and his old task-oriented style which has the force of habit behind it.

This idea was supported in a study the General Electric Company conducted at one of its turbine and generator plants.[112] In this study the leadership styles of about ninety foremen were analyzed and rated as "democratic," "authoritarian," or "mixed." In discussing the findings, Saul W. Gellerman reported that:

> The lowest morale in the plant was found among those men whose foremen were rated *between* the democratic and authoritarian extremes. The GE research team felt that these foremen may have varied inconsistently in their tactics, permissive at one moment and hardfisted the next, in a way that left their men frustrated and unable to anticipate how they would be treated. The naturally autocratic supervisor who is exposed to human relations training may behave in exactly such a manner . . . a pattern which will probably make him even harder to work for than he was before being "enlightened." [113]

In summary, changing the style of managers is a difficult process, and one that takes considerable time. Expecting miracles overnight will only lead to frustration and uneasiness for both managers and their subordinates. Consequently, we recommend that change in overall management style in an organization should be planned and implemented on a long-term basis so that expectations can be realistic for all involved.

Changes in Expectations Vs. Changes in Personality

Using the feedback model appearing in Chapter Two, we can begin to explain why it is so difficult to make changes in leader personality in the short-run.

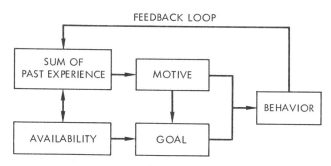

FIGURE 6.4 Feedback model.

As discussed earlier, when a person behaves in a motivating situation, his behavior becomes a new input to his inventory of past experience. The earlier in life that this input occurs, the greater its potential effect on future behavior. At that time, this behavior represents a larger portion of the individual's total past experience than the same behavior input would later in life. In addition, the longer a behavior is reinforced, the more patterned it becomes and the more difficult it is to change. That is why it is easier to make personality changes early in life. As a person gets older, more time and new experiences are necessary to effect a change in behavior. Consider Steve, the general foreman, who must make a decision about a new job. If he had come out of college without prior reinforcement for any particular management style and been using a task-oriented style on a production line for six months to a year, it would not be too difficult for a company to make some appropriate changes in his style to accommodate the relationship demands of a new position. However, he has had fifteen years of reinforcement using a task-oriented style. Therefore, while it is possible to change his behavior, it will be difficult to accomplish, except over a long period of time under conducive conditions. It almost becomes a matter of economics. How much can be invested in implementing such a change?

As was discussed in Chapter One, changes in behavior are much more difficult and time-consuming than changes in knowledge and attitudes. Since changes in expectations, in reality, are changes in knowledge and attitudes, these can be implemented more rapidly than changes in personality. In fact, changes in expectations may be accomplished merely by having the leader sit down and clarify what his behavior will be with the individuals involved. Once they understand his style they can more easily adjust their expectations to it. This is easier than attempting the tedious task of changing his basic personality.

Selection of Key Subordinates

It may be important to point out that it is not always necessary for superiors and subordinates within an organization to have similar styles. People don't have to have the same personalities to be compatible. What is necessary is that they share perceptions of each other's roles and have common goals and objectives. It is often more appropriate for a manager to recruit key subordinates who can compensate for areas in which he has short-comings, than to surround himself with aides who are all alike. For example, Henry Ford, who was considered a paternalistic leader, placed in key positions in the organization men who supplemented him, rather than duplicated his style. Henry Bennett, for one, acted as a "hatchet-man," clearing deadwood from the organization (high task). Another subordinate acted as a confidant to Henry (high relationships). While these styles differed considerably, Ford's success during that time was based on compatibility of expectations; each understood the other's role and was committed to common goals and objectives.

Changing Situational Elements

Recognizing some of the limitations of training and development programs which concentrate only on changing leadership styles, Fiedler has suggested that "It would seem more promising at this time to teach the individual to recognize the conditions under which he can perform best and to modify the situation to suit his leadership style." [114] This philosophy, which he calls "organizational engineering," is based on the assumption: "It is almost always easier to change a man's work environment than it is to change his personality or his style of relating to others." [115] While we basically agree with Fiedler's assumption, we want to make it clear that we feel change in both are difficult, but possible. In many cases, the best strategy might be to attempt to make some changes in his style and expectations and some changes in the other elements of his situation, rather than concentrating on one or the other.

Fiedler is helpful, though, in suggesting ways in which a leadership situation could be modified to fit the leader's style. These suggestions are based on his Leadership Contingency Model which we discussed in the last chapter. As you recall, Fiedler feels there are three major situational variables which seem to determine whether a given situation is favorable or unfavorable to a leader: (1) *leader-member relations*—his personal relations with the members of his group, (2) *position power*—the power and authority which his position provides and (3) *task structure*—the degree of structure (routine vs. challenging) in the task which the group has been assigned to perform. The changes in each of these variables which Fiedler recommends can be expressed in task or relationship terms; each change tends to favor either a task-oriented or a relationships-oriented leader,[116] as illustrated in Table 6.2, page 112.

With changes like these, Fiedler suggests that the situational elements confronting a leader can be modified to fit his style. He recognized though, as we have been arguing, that the success of organizational engineering depends on training an individual to be able to diagnose his own leader personality or style and the other environmental variables. Only when he has accurately interpreted these variables can he determine whether any changes are necessary. If changes are needed, the leader does not necessarily have to initiate any in his own particular situation. He might prefer to transfer to a situation which better fits his style. In this new environment no immediate changes may be necessary.

INCREASING EFFECTIVENESS

We have been discussing possible changes that could be made in leadership style or expectations and some of the situational elements. We want to focus our attention now on specifically making changes in reference to our own culture.

VARIABLE BEING CHANGED	CHANGE MADE	
	STYLE FAVORS	
	TASK	RELATIONSHIPS
LEADER-MEMBER RELATIONS	The leader could be given: 1) Followers who are quite different from him in a number of ways. 2) Followers who are notorious for their conflict.	The leader could be given: 1) Followers who are very similar to him in attitude, opinion, technical background, race, etc. 2) Followers who generally get along well with their superiors.
POSITION POWER OF THE LEADER	The leader could be given: 1) High rank and corresponding recognition, i.e., a vice-presidency. 2) Followers who are two or three ranks below him. 3) Followers who are dependent upon their leader for guidance and instruction. 4) Final authority in making all the decisions for the group. 5) All information about organizational plans, thus making him an expert in his group.	The leader could be given: 1) Little rank (office) or official recognition. 2) Followers who are equal to him in rank. 3) Followers who are experts in their field and are independent of their leader. 4) No authority in making decisions for the group. 5) No more information about organizational plans than his followers get, placing him on an equal "footing" with them.
TASK STRUCTURE	The leader could be given: 1) A structured production task which has specific instructions on what he and his followers should do.	The leader could be given: 1) An unstructured policy-making task which has no prescribed operating procedures.

TABLE 6.2   Changes in the leadership situation expressed in terms of task and relationships.

Need Satisfaction in the United States

In our culture, we have a comparatively high level of education and standard of living and thus, a large majority of our population, in Maslow's terms,[117] now have their basic physiological and safety-

112

security needs fairly satisfied. Management can no longer depend on the satisfaction of these needs, through pay, incentive plans, hospitalization, etc., as primary motivating factors which influence industrial employees. In our society today, there is almost a built-in expectation in people that physiological and safety needs will be fulfilled. In fact, in our society people do not generally have to worry about where their next meal will come from or whether they will be protected from the elements or physical danger. They are now more susceptible to motivation from other needs: People want to belong, be recognized as "somebody," and have a chance to develop to their fullest potential. As William H. Haney has said:

> The managerial practice, therefore, should be geared to the subordinate's *current level of maturity with the overall goal of helping him to develop, to require progressively less external control, and to gain more and more self-control.* And why would a man want this? Because under these conditions he achieves satisfaction on the job at the levels, primarily the ego and self-fulfillment levels, at which he is the most *motivatable.*[118]

This concept is illustrated in Figure 6.5.

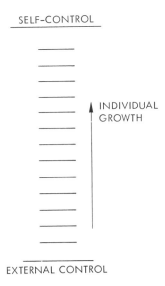

SELF-CONTROL

INDIVIDUAL GROWTH

EXTERNAL CONTROL

FIGURE 6.5 Balance of external and self-control.

This shift in the need disposition of our general population has a tremendous influence on current research findings. As you will recall, Likert found that employee-centered supervisors who use general supervision tend to have higher producing sections than job-centered supervisors who use close supervision. We underline the word "tend" because we recognize this in our society, yet we also realize there are exceptions to this tendency which are even evident in Likert's data. What Likert found was that a subordinate generally responds well to a superior's high expectations and genuine confidence in him and tries to justify his boss's expectations of him. His resulting high performance will reinforce his superior's high trust for him, for it is easy to trust and respect the man who meets or exceeds your expectations. This occurrence could be called the effective cycle.

FIGURE 6.6   Effective cycle.

Yet, as we have pointed out earlier, the concentration on output variables, as a means of evaluating effectiveness, tends to lead to short-run, task-oriented leader behavior. This style, in some cases, does not allow much room for a trusting relationship with employees. Instead, subordinates are told what to do and how to do it, with little consideration expressed for their ideas or feelings. After a while, the subordinates respond with minimal effort and resentment; low performance results in these instances. Reinforced by low expectations, it becomes a vicious cycle. Many other examples could be given which result in this all too common problem in organizations as shown in Figure 6.7.

FIGURE 6.7   Ineffective cycle.

Breaking the Ineffective Cycle

The question is how do we break this ineffective cycle and make it effective? There are at least two alternatives available to both the subordinate and the superior.

The subordinate can either leave this job and seek a situation in which his superior will have higher expectations of his performance or he can respond to low expectations and trust with high performance, thus hoping to eventually gain the respect of his superior and change his expectations.

The superior can either fire the subordinate and hire someone who he expects to perform well or respond to low performance with high expectations and trust.

The latter choice for both the subordinate and the superior is difficult. In effect, the attempt is to change the expectations or behavior of the other. It is especially difficult for a superior to change expectations about someone who has shown no indication that he deserves to be trusted. The key, then, is to change appropriately. When an individual's performance is low, one cannot expect drastic changes overnight, regardless of changes in expectations or other incentives. The key is often reinforcing positively *successive approximations*. By successive approximations is meant behavior that comes closer and closer to our expectations of good performance. Similar to the child learning some new behavior, we do not expect high levels of performance at the outset. So, as a parent or teacher, we would use positive reinforcement as the child's behavior approaches the desired level of performance. Therefore, the manager must be aware of any progress of his subordinate, so he is in a position to reinforce appropriately this change.

As a supervisor, you must get to know your employees to determine which ones can be expected to handle general supervision and which ones cannot. But where appropriate, high expectations and trust tends to produce favorable results in our culture. The hope is that through the establishment of this type of relationship, the employee will have the freedom to satisfy both motivation and hygiene needs while at the same time striving for organizational objectives. This is what McGregor calls a true "integration of goals." [119]

To illustrate this concept we can divide an organization into two groups, management and employees. The respective goals of these two groups and the resultant attainment of the goals of the organization to which they belong are illustrated in Figure 6.8.

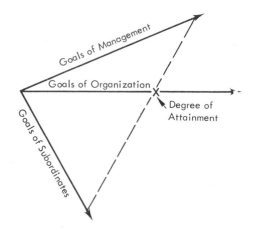

FIGURE 6.8 Directions of goals of management,
subordinates, and the organization—
moderate organizational accomplishment.

In this instance, the goals of management are somewhat compatible with the goals of the organization, but are not exactly the same. On the other hand, the goals of the subordinates are almost at odds with those of the organization. The result of the interaction between the goals of management and subordinates is a compromise and actual performance is a combination of both. It is at this approximate point that the degree of attainment of the goals of the organization can be pictured. This situation could be much worse where there is little accomplishment of organizational goals as illustrated in Figure 6.9.

In this situation, there seems to be a general disregard for the welfare of the organization. Both managers and workers see their own goals conflicting with the organization's. Consequently, both morale and performance will tend to be low and organizational accomplishment will be negligible. In some cases, the organizational goals can be so opposed that no positive progress is obtained. The result often is substantial losses, or draining off of assets. (See Figure 6.10.) In fact, organizations are going out of business every day because of these very reasons.

The hope in an organization is to create a climate in which one of two things occurs. The individuals in the organization (both managers and workers) either perceive their goals as being the same as the

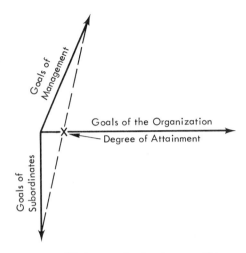

FIGURE 6.9 Little organizational accomplishment.

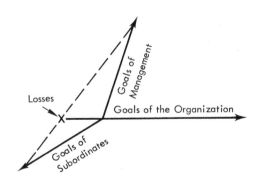

FIGURE 6.10 No positive organizational accomplishment.

goals of the organization, or, although different, they see their own goals being satisfied as a direct result of working for the goals of the organization. Consequently, the closer we can get the individual's goals and objectives to the organization's goals, the greater will be the organizational performance as illustrated in Figure 6.11.

FIGURE 6.11   An integration of the goals of
management, subordinates, and
the organization—*high* organizational accomplishment.

One of the ways in which the effective leader bridges the gap between the individual's and the organization's goals is by creating a
loyalty to himself among his men. He does this by being an influ-
ential spokesman for them with higher management.[120]

The leader then has no difficulty in communicating organizational
goals to his men and his men do not find it difficult to associate the
acceptance of these goals with accomplishment of their own need
satisfaction.

Management by Objectives

We realize that it is not an easy task to integrate the goals and
objectives of all individuals with the goals of the organization. Yet
it is not an impossible task. An approach to this problem which has
been used successfully in some organizations in our culture is a process
called *management by objectives*.

Management by objectives is basically:

A process whereby the superior and the subordinate managers of an
enterprise jointly, identify its common goals, define each individual's major areas of responsibility in terms of the results expected
of him, and use these measures as guides for operating the unit and
assessing the contribution of each of its members.[121]

This process in some cases has been successfully carried beyond the managerial level to include hourly employees. A number of companies including Non-Linear Systems Inc., and Union Carbide have had significant success in broadening individual responsibility and involvement in work planning at the lowest organizational levels.[122] The concept rests on a philosophy of management which emphasizes an integration between external control (by managers) and self-control (by subordinates). It can apply to any manager or individual no matter what his level or function, and to any organization, regardless of size.

The smooth functioning of this system is an agreement between a manager and his subordinate about his own or his group's performance goals during a stated time period. These goals can emphasize either output variables or intervening variables, or some combination of both. The important thing is that goals are jointly established and agreed upon in advance. This is then followed by a review of the subordinate's performance in relation to accepted goals at the end of the time period. Both superior and subordinate participate in this review and any other evaluation which takes place. It has been found that objectives that are formulated with each person participating seem to gain more acceptance than those imposed by an authority figure in the organization. Consultation and participation in this area tends to establish personal risk for the attainment of the formulated objective by those who actually perform the task.

Prior to setting individual objectives, the common goals of the entire organization should be clarified, and, at this time, any appropriate changes in the organizational structure should be made: changes in titles, duties, relationships, authority, responsibility, span of control, etc.

Throughout the time period what is to be accomplished by the entire organization should be compared with what is being accomplished; necessary adjustments should be made and inappropriate goals discarded. At the end of the time period, a final mutual review of objectives and performance takes place. If there is a discrepancy between the two, efforts are initiated to determine what steps can be taken to overcome these problems. This sets the stage for the determination of objectives for the next time period.

The entire cycle of management by objectives is represented graphically in Figure 6.12.[123]

Management by objectives may become a powerful tool in gaining mutual commitment and high productivity for an organization, where management realizes this type of involvement of subordinates is appropriate in its situation.

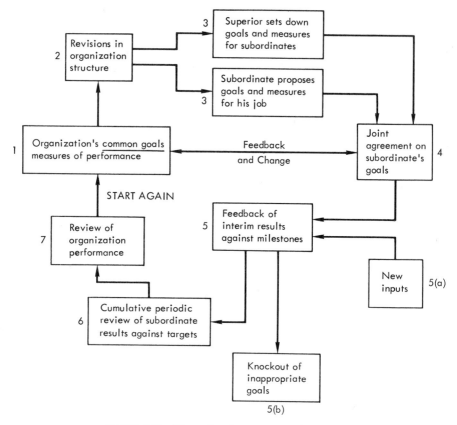

FIGURE 6.12 The cycle of management by objectives.

CONCLUSIONS

There is still much unknown about human behavior. Unanswered questions remain and further research is necessary. Knowledge about motivation and leader behavior will continue to be of great concern to practitioners of management for several reasons: It can help improve the effective utilization of human resources; it can help in preventing resistance to change, restriction of output, and labor disputes; and often it can lead to a more profitable organization.

Our intention has been to provide a conceptual framework that may be useful to the reader in applying the conclusions of the behavioral sciences. The value a framework of this kind has is *not* in changing one's knowledge, but comes when it is applied in changing one's behavior in working with people.

Notes

1. Elton Mayo, *The Social Problems of an Industrial Civilization* (Boston: Harvard Business School, 1945), p. 23.

2. *Ibid.*, p. 20.

3. See as examples, Harold Koontz and Cyril O'Donnell, *Principles of Management*, fourth edition (New York: McGraw-Hill Book Co., Inc., 1968): and William H. Newman, Charles E. Summer, and E. Kirby Warren, *The Process of Management* (Englewood Cliffs, New Jersey: Prentice-Hall, Inc., 1967).

4. Koontz and O'Donnell, *Principles of Management*, p. 54.

5. These descriptions were adopted from a classification developed by Robert L. Katz, "Skills of an Effective Administrator," *Harvard Business Review* (January-February 1955), pp. 33-42.

6. John D. Rockefeller as quoted in Garret L. Bergen and William V. Haney, *Organizational Relations and Management Action* (New York: McGraw-Hill Book Co., 1966), p. 3.

7. Data as reported in Bergen and Haney, *Organizational Relations and Management Action*.

8. Sigmund Freud, *The Ego and the Id* (London: Hogarth Press, 1927) and *New Introductory Lectures on Psychoanalysis* (New York: Norton, 1933).

9. Abraham H. Maslow, *Motivation and Personality* (New York: Harper and Brothers, 1954).

10. Maslow, "A Theory of Human Motivation," *Psychological Review,* Vol. 50, 1943, pp. 388-389.

11. Saul W. Gellerman, *Motivation and Productivity* (New York: American Management Association, 1963). See also Gellerman, *Management by Motivation* (New York: American Management Association, 1968).

12. Peter F. Drucker, "How to be an Employee" *Psychology Today,* March 1968, a reprint from Fortune Magazine.

13. Gellerman, *Motivation and Productivity,* pp. 154-155.

14. Stanley Schacter, *The Psychology of Affiliation* (Stanford, California: Stanford University Press, 1959).

15. Mayo, *The Social Problems of an Industrial Civilization;* see also Mayo, *The Human Problems of an Industrial Civilization* (New York: Macmillan Co., 1933).

16. Vance Packard, *The Status Seekers* (New York: David McKay Company, Inc., 1959).

17. David Riesman, *The Lonely Crowd* (New Haven, Conn.: Yale University Press, 1950).

18. Gellerman, *Motivation and Productivity,* p. 151.

19. *Ibid.,* pp. 150-154.

20. Alfred Adler, *Social Interest* (London: Faber and Faber, 1938). See also H. L. Ansbacher and R. R. Ansbacher (editors), *The Individual Psychology of Alfred Adler* (New York: Basic Books, Inc., Publishing, 1956).

21. Robert W. White, "Motivation Reconsidered: The Concept of Competence," *Psychological Review,* Vol. 66, No. 5, 1959.

22. David C. McClelland, J. W. Atkinson, R. A. Clark, and E. L. Lowell, *The Achievement Motive* (New York: Appleton-Century-Crofts, Inc., 1953) and *The Achieving Society* (Princeton, N.J.: D. Van Nostrand Co., 1961).

23. William F. Whyte, *Money and Motivation* (New York: Harper and Row, Publishers, Inc., 1955).

24. Gellerman, *Motivation and Productivity,* pp. 160-169.

25. For detailed descriptions of this research see: F. J. Roethlisberger and W. J. Dickson, *Management and the Worker* (Cambridge: Harvard University Press, 1939); T. N. Whitehead, *The Industrial Worker,* 2 Vols. (Cambridge: Harvard University Press, 1938); Mayo, *The Human Problems of an Industrial Civilization.*

26. Mayo, *The Social Problems of an Industrial Civilization,* pp. 34-56.

27. Douglas McGregor, *The Human Side of Enterprise* (McGraw-Hill Book Co., Inc., New York, 1960). See also McGregor, *Leadership and Motivation* (Boston, Mass.: MIT Press, 1966).

28. Chris Argyris, *Personality and Organization* (New York: Harper and Row, Publishers, Inc., 1957); *Interpersonal Competence and Organizational Effectiveness* (Homewood, Ill.: Dorsey Press, 1962); and *Integrating the Individual and the Organization* (New York: Wiley, 1964).

29. N. Breman, *The Making of a Moron* (New York: Sheed and Ward, 1953).

30. Frederick Herzberg, Bernard Mausner and Barbara Synderman, *The*

Motivation to Work (New York: John Wiley, 1959) and Herzberg, *Work and the Nature of Man* (New York: World Publishing Co., 1966).

31. Herzberg, Mausner, and Synderman, *The Motivation to Work*, p. ix.
32. Rensis Likert, *The Human Organization* (New York: McGraw-Hill Book Co., 1967); see also Likert, *New Patterns of Management* (New York: McGraw-Hill, 1961).
33. Descriptions adapted from Likert, *The Human Organization*, pp. 4-10.
34. *Ibid.*
35. A. J. Marrow, D. G. Bowers and S. E. Seashore (eds.), *Management by Participation* (New York: Harper and Row, 1967).
36. Peter F. Drucker, *The Practice of Management* (New York: Harper and Row, Publishers, 1954).
37. George R. Terry, *Principles of Management*, third edition (Homewood, Illinois: Richard D. Irwin, Inc., 1960), p. 5.
38. Terry, *Principles of Management*, p. 493.
39. Robert Tannenbaum, Irving R. Weschler and Fred Massarik, *Leadership and Organization: A Behavioral Science Approach* (New York: McGraw-Hill Book Company, Inc., 1959).
40. Koontz and O'Donnell, *Principles of Management*, Second Edition, p. 435.
41. Cecil A. Gibb, "Leadership" in *Handbook of Social Psychology*, Gardner Lindzey (ed.) (Cambridge, Mass.: Addison-Wesley Publishing Co., Inc., 1954). See also Roger M. Stogdill, "Personal Factors Associated with Leadership: A Survey of the Literature," *Journal of Psychology*, 25, 1948, pp. 35-71.
42. Eugene E. Jennings, "The Anatomy of Leadership," *Management of Personnel Quarterly*, I, No. 1 (Autumn 1961).
43. John K. Hemphill, *Situational Factors in Leadership*, Monograph No. 32 (Columbus, Ohio: Bureau of Educational Research, The Ohio State University, 1949).
44. Chester I. Barnard, *The Functions of the Executive* (Cambridge, Mass.: Harvard University Press, 1938).
45. Frederick W. Taylor, *The Principles of Scientific Management* (New York: Harper and Brothers, 1911).
46. Mayo, *The Social Problems of an Industrial Civilization*.
47. Robert Tannenbaum and Warren H. Schmidt, "How to Choose a Leadership Pattern" *Harvard Business Review*, March-April, 1957, pp. 95-101.
48. Roger M. Stogdill and Alvin E. Coons (eds.), *Leader Behavior: Its Description and Measurement*, Research Monograph No. 88 (Columbus, Ohio: Bureau of Business Research, The Ohio State University, 1957).
49. Andrew W. Halpin, *The Leadership Behavior of School Superintendents* (Chicago: Midwest Administration Center, The University of Chicago, 1959), p. 4.
50. D. Katz, N. Maccoby and Nancy C. Morse, *Productivity, Supervision, and Morale in an Office Situation* (Detroit, Michigan: The Darel Press, Inc., 1950); D. Katz, N. Maccoby, G. Gurin, and Lucretia G. Floor, *Produc-*

tivity, Supervision and Morale Among Railroad Workers (Ann Arbor, Michigan: Survey Research Center, 1951).

51. Dorwin Cartwright and Alvin Zander, *Group Dynamics: Research and Theory* (Evanston, Illinois: Row Peterson and Co., 1960).

52. *Ibid.,* p. 496.

53. *Ibid.*

54. Robert R. Blake and Jane S. Mouton, *The Managerial Grid* (Houston, Texas: Gulf Publishing, 1964).

55. Robert R. Blake *et al.,* "Breakthrough in Organization Development," *Harvard Business Review* (November-December 1964), p. 136.

56. Barnard, *The Functions of the Executive.*

57. Warren G. Bennis, "Leadership Theory and Administrative Behavior: The Problems of Authority," *Administrative Science Quarterly,* IV, No. 3 (December, 1959), p. 274.

58. Halpin, *The Leadership Behavior of School Superintendents,* p. 79.

59. *Ibid.*

60. *Ibid.,* p. 6.

61. Blake *et al.,* "Breakthrough . . . ," p. 135.

62. Likert, *New Patterns of Management,* p. 7.

63. *Ibid.*

64. *Ibid.,* p. 9.

65. *Ibid.*

66. Paul Hersey, an unpublished research project, 1965.

67. Koontz and O'Donnell, *Principles of Management.*

68. Paul Hersey, *Management Concepts and Behavior: Programmed Instruction for Managers* (Little Rock, Arkansas: Marvern Publishing Co., 1967), p. 15.

69. Fred E. Fiedler, *A Theory of Leadership Effectiveness* (New York: Mc-Graw-Hill Book Company, 1967).

70. *Ibid.,* p. 13.

71. Adapted from Fiedler, *A Theory of Leadership Effectiveness,* p. 14.

72. Since our model is an outgrowth of the Ohio State Leadership Studies these definitions have been adapted from their definitions of "Initiating Structure" (task) and "Consideration" (relationships), Stogdill and Coons, *Leader Behavior: Its Description and Measurement,* pp. 42-43.

73. William J. Reddin, "The 3-D Management Style Theory," *Training and Development Journal* (April 1967), pp. 8-17. See also Reddin, "The 3-D Story," *Executive,* January 1967, Vol. 9, No. 1.

74. Reddin, "The 3-D Management Style Theory," p. 13.

75. Parts of this table were adapted from the Managerial style descriptions of William J. Reddin, *The 3-D Management Style Theory,* Theory Paper #2—Managerial Styles. (Frederichton, N.B. Canada: Social Science Systems, 1967), pp. 5-6.

76. W. J. Reddin's 3-D Management Style Theory seems to be attitudinal in nature rather than behavioral. The dimensions of his model are task orientation and relationships orientation. See Reddin, "The 3-D Management Style Theory," *Training and Development Journal.*

77. Amitai Etzioni, *A Comparative Analysis of Complex Organizations* (New York: The Free Press of Glencoe, 1961).

78. Fiedler, *A Theory of Leadership Effectiveness*, p. 9.

79. Reddin, "The 3-D Management Style Theory." This is one of the critical differences between Reddin's 3-D Management Style Theory and the Tri-Dimensional Leader Effectiveness Model. Reddin in his model seems to consider only output variables in determining effectiveness while in the Tri-Dimensional Leader Effectiveness Model both intervening variables and output variables are taken into consideration.

80. Likert, *New Patterns of Management*, p. 2.

81. L. Coch and J. R. P. French, "Overcoming Resistance to Change" in Cartwright and Zander (eds.) *Group Dynamics: Research and Theory.*

82. See Kurt Lewin "Group Decision and Social Change" in G. Swanson, T. Newcomb and E. Hartley (eds.) *Readings in Social Psychology* (New York: Henry Holt, 1952) pp. 459-473; K. Lewin, R. Lippitt and R. White "Leader Behavior and Member Reaction in Three 'Social Climates'" in Cartwright and Zander (eds.) *Group Dynamics* . . . pp. 485-611; and N. Morse and E. Reimer, "The Experimental Change of a Major Organizational Variable," *Journal of Abnormal Social Psychology,* 52 (1956) pp. 120-129.

83. John P. French, Jr., Joachim Israel and Dagfinn As, "An Experiment on Participation in a Norwegian Factory" *Human Relations,* 13 (1960), pp. 3-19.

84. A. K. Korman, " 'Consideration,' 'Initiating Structure,' and Organizational Criteria—A review," *Personnel Psychology: A Journal of Applied Research,* Vol. 19, No. 4 (Winter, 1966), pp. 349-361.

85. *Ibid.,* p. 360.

86. Fiedler, *A Theory of Leadership Effectiveness*, p. 247.

87. See C. A. Gibb, "Leadership," in *Handbook of Social Psychology,* Gardner Lindzey, ed. (Cambridge, Mass.: Addison Wesley Publishing Co., Inc., 1964). A. P. Hare, *Handbook of Small Group Research* (New York: John Wiley, 1965); and D. C. Pelz, "Leadership Within a Hierarchial Organization," *Journal of Social Issues,* 1961, 7, pp. 49-55.

88. Reddin, "The 3-D Management Style Theory," *Training and Development Journal* (April, 1967).

89. Reddin, *The 3-D Management Style Theory,* Theory Paper #8—Concept Dictionary (Frederichton, N.B. Canada: Social Science Systems, 1967) p. 4.

90. These environmental variables have been adapted from a list of situational elements discussed by Reddin in *3-D Management Style Theory,* Theory Paper No. 5—Diagnostic Skill, p. 2.

91. J. W. Getzels and E. G. Guba, "Social Behavior and the Administrative Process." *The School Review,* Vol. 65, No. 4 (Winter 1957), pp. 423-441.

92. Leland P. Bradford, Jack R. Gibb and Kenneth D. Benne, *T-Group Theory and Laboratory Method* (New York: John Wiley and Sons, Inc., 1964).

93. Warren G. Bennis, *Changing Organizations* (New York: McGraw-Hill Book Company, 1966), p. 120.

94. Chris Argyris, "We Must Make Work Worthwhile," *Life*, Vol. 62, No. 18 (May 5, 1967), p. 66.

95. *Ibid.*

96. See Chris Argyris "T-Groups for Organization Effectiveness," *Harvard Business Review*, Vol. 42 (1964), pp. 60-74; Edgar H. Schein and Warren G. Bennis, *Personal and Organization Change Through Group Methods* (New York: John Wiley and Sons, Inc., 1965). Robert R. Blake et al. "Breakthrough in Organization Development," *Harvard Business Review* (November-December 1964) and Chris Argyris, *Interpersonal Competence and Organizational Effectiveness* (Homewood, Illinois: Dorsey Press, 1962).

97. Fillmore H. Sanford, *Authoritarianism and Leadership* (Philadelphia: Institute for Research in Human Relations, 1950).

98. Victor H. Vroom, *Some Personality Determinants of the Effects of Participation* (Englewood Cliffs, New Jersey: Prentice-Hall, Inc., 1960).

99. Gellerman, *Motivation and Productivity*.

100. Reddin, *3-D Management Style Theory*, Theory Paper #5—Diagnostic Skill, p. 4.

101. William E. Henry, "The Business Executive: The Psychodynamics of a Social Role," *The American Journal of Sociology*, Vol. 54, No. 4, January 1949, pp. 286-291.

102. Reddin, Theory Paper #5—Diagnostic Skill, p. 4.

103. Waino W. Suojanen, *The Dynamics of Management* (New York: Holt, Rinehart and Winston, 1966).

104. Fiedler, *A Theory of Leadership Effectiveness*.

105. Victor H. Vroom and Floyd C. Mann, "Leader Authoritarianism and Employee Attitudes," *Personnel Psychology*, Summer 1960.

106. Reddin, *The 3-D Management Style Theory*, Theory Paper #6, "Style Flex" (Frederichton, N.B. Canada: Social Science Systems, 1967), p. 4.

107. Reddin, Theory Paper #6—Style Flex, p. 6.

108. Reddin, Theory Paper #5—Diagnostic Skills, p. 6.

109. Adapted from Reddin, Theory Paper #6—Style Flex, p. 6.

110. Fiedler, *A Theory of Leadership Effectiveness*, p. 248.

111. Likert, *New Patterns of Management*, p. 248.

112. *Leadership Style and Employee Morale* (New York: General Electric Company, Public and Employee Relations Services, 1959).

113. Gellerman, *Motivation and Productivity*, p. 43.

114. Fiedler, *A Theory of Leadership Effectiveness*, p. 255.

115. *Ibid.*

116. This figure was adapted from Fiedler's discussion in *A Theory of Leadership Effectiveness*, p. 255-256.

117. Maslow, *Motivation and Personality*.

118. William H. Haney, *Communication and Organizational Behavior: Text and Cases*, Revised Edition (Homewood, Illinois: Richard D. Irwin, Inc., 1967), p. 20.

119. McGregor, *The Human Side of Enterprise*.

120. Gellerman, *Motivation and Productivity*, p. 265.

121. George S. Odiorne, *Management by Objectives* (New York: Pitman Publishing Corporation, 1965).

122. Argyris, *Integrating the Individual and the Organization;* Maslow *Eupsychian Management* (Homewood, Illinois: Richard D. Irwin, Inc. and Dorsey Press, 1965).

123. Odiorne, *Management by Objectives*, p. 78.

Selected
Bibliography

Ansbacher, K. L., and R. R. Ansbacher (eds.), *The Individual Psychology of Alfred Adler* (New York: Basic Books, Inc., Publishing, 1956).

Applewhite, Phillip, *Organizational Behavior* (Englewood Cliffs, New Jersey: Prentice-Hall, Inc., 1965).

Arendt, Hannah, *The Human Condition* (Chicago: University of Chicago Press, 1958).

Arensburg, C. M., and D. McGregor, Determination of morale in an industrial company. *Applied.Anthropology*, 1942, 1 (2), 12-34.

Argyle, Michael, Godfrey Gardner and Frank Cioffi. Supervisory methods related to productivity and absenteeism, and labor turnover. *Human Relations*, 1958, 11, 23-40.

Argyris, Chris, *Executive Leadership: An Appraisal of a Manager in Action* (Hamden, Conn.: Shoe String Press, Inc., 1953).

————, *Integrating the Individual and the Organization* (New York: John Wiley, 1964).

————, *Interpersonal Competence and Organizational Effectiveness* (Homewood, Illinois: Dorsey Press and Richard D. Irwin, Inc., 1962).

————, *Organization and Innovation* (Homewood, Ill.: Dorsey Press and Richard D. Irwin, Inc., 1965).

————, *Personality and Organization* (New York: Harper and Row, Publishers, 1957).

————, "T-Groups for organization effectiveness," *Harvard Business Review,* 42, 1964.

Asch, S., *Social Psychology* (Englewood Cliffs, New Jersey: Prentice-Hall, 1952).

Ashby, W. Ross, *An Introduction to Cybernetics* (London: Chapman and Hall, Ltd., 1956).

Barnard, Chester I., *The Functions of the Executive* (Cambridge, Mass.: Harvard University Press, 1938).

Bass, Bernard M., *Leadership, Psychology and Organizational Behavior* (New York: Harper and Row, 1960).

————, *Organization and Management* (Cambridge, Mass.: Harvard University, 1948).

————, Margaret W. Pryer, Eugene L. Gaier and Austin W. Flint, Interacting effects of control, motivation, group practice, and problem difficulty on attempted leadership. *Journal of Abnormal and Social Psychology,* 1958, 56, 352-358.

Baumgartel, H. J., Jr., Leadership motivation and attitudes in research laboratories. *Journal of Social Issues,* 1956, 12 (2), 24-31.

Bavelas, A. Communication patterns in task-oriented groups. In D. Cartwright and A. Zander (eds.), *Group Dynamics.* (Evanston, Illinois: Row, Peterson, 1953).

Beer, Michael, Robert Buckhout, Milton W. Horowitz, and Seymour Levy, Some perceived properties of the difference between leaders and nonleaders. *The Journal of Psychology,* 1959, 47, 49-56.

Bell, Graham B. and Robert L. French, Consistency of individual leadership position in small groups of varying membership. *Journal of Abnormal and Social Psychology,* 1950, 45, 764-767.

Bendix, R., *Work and Authority in Industry.* (New York: John Wiley, 1956).

Benne, Kenneth D. and Paul Sheats. Functional roles of group members. *Journal of Social Issues,* 1948, 4 (2), 41-49.

Bennis, Warren G., *Changing Organizations* (New York: McGraw-Hill Book Company, 1966).

————, Leadership theory and administrative behavior: the problem of authority, *Administrative Science Quarterly,* IV, No. 3 (December 1959), 259-301.

Berelson, Bernard, and Gary A. Steiner, *Human Behavior: An Inventory of Scientific Findings* (New York: Harcourt, Brace and World, 1964).

Bergen, Garret L. and William V. Haney, *Organizational Relations and Management Action* (New York: McGraw-Hill Book Company, 1966).

Blake, Robert R., *et. al.*, Breakthrough in organization development, *Harvard Business Review* (November-December 1964).

Blake, Robert R. and Jane S. Mouton, *The Managerial Grid* (Houston, Texas: Gulf Publishing, 1964).

Blau, Peter M., *The Dynamics of Bureaucracy* (Chicago: The University of Chicago Press, 1955).

Blum, F. H., *Toward a Democratic Work Process* (New York: Harper and Row, 1953).

Borg, Walter R. The behavior of emergent and designated leaders in situational tests. *Sociometry*, 1957, 20, 95-104.

——— and Ernst C. Tupes, Personality characteristics related to leadership behavior in two types of small group situational problems. *Journal of Applied Psychology*, 1958, 42, 252-256.

Borgatta, Edgar F., Robert F. Bales, and Arthur S. Couch, Some findings relevant to the great man theory of leadership. *American Sociological Review*, 1954, 19, 755-759.

Bowers, D. G. and S. E. Seashore. Predicting organizational effectiveness with a four-factor theory of leadership. *Administrative Science Quarterly*, 1966, 11 (2), 238-263.

Bradford, Leland P., Jack R. Gibb and Kenneth D. Benne, *T-Group Theory and Laboratory Method* (New York: John Wiley, 1964).

Breman, N., *The Making of a Moron* (New York: Sheed and Ward, 1953).

Brooks, E., What successful executives do. *Personnel*, 1955, 32 (3), 210-225.

Brown, J. A. C., *The Social Psychology of Industry* (London: Penguin Books, 1954).

Browne, C. G. and B. J. Neitzel, Communication, supervision and morale. *Journal of Applied Psychology*, 1952, 36, 86-91.

Browne, C. G. and Richard P. Shore, Leadership and predictive abstracting. *Journal of Applied Psychology*, 1956, 40, 112-116.

Carlson, Richard O., *Executive Succession and Organizational Change* (Chicago: Mid-West Administration Center, University of Chicago, 1962).

Carp, Francis M., Bart M. Vitola and Frank L. McLanathan, Human relations knowledge and social distance set in supervisors. *Journal of Applied Psychology*, 1963, 47, 78-90.

Carter, Lauhor, William Haythorn and Margaret Howell, A further investigation of the criteria of leadership. *Journal of Abnormal and Social Psychology*, 1950, 45, 350-358.

Cartwright, D., Achieving change in people: some applications of group dynamics theory. *Human Relations*, 1951, 4, 381-392.

———, The potential contribution of graph theory to organization theory. In M. Haire (ed.), *Modern Organization Theory* (New York: John Wiley, 1959).

———, and R. Lippitt, Group dynamics and the individual. *International Journal of Group Psychotherapy,* 1957, 7 (1), 86-102.

———, and A. Zander (eds.), *Group Dynamics: Research and Theory* (2nd ed.) (Evanston, Ill.: Row, Peterson, 1960).

Cattell, Raymond B. New concepts for measuring leadership in terms of group syntality. *Human Relations,* 1951, 4, 161-184.

Chowdhry, Kamla and Theodore M. Newcomb. The relative abilities of leaders and non-leaders to estimate opinions of their own groups. *Journal of Abnormal and Social Psychology,* 1952, 47, 51-57.

Christner, Charlotte A. and John K. Hemphill, Leader behavior of B-29 commanders and changes in crew members' attitudes toward the crew. *Sociometry,* 1955, 18, 82-87.

Coates, Charles H. and Roland J. Pellegrin, Executives and supervisors: informal factors in differential bureaucratic promotion. *Administrative Science Quarterly,* 1957, 2, 200-215.

———, Executives and supervisors: contrasting self-conceptions of each other. *American Sociological Review,* 1957, 22, 217-220.

Coch, L. and J. R. P. French, Jr., Overcoming resistance to change. *Human Relations,* 1948, 1 (4), 512-532.

Comrey, A. L., W. S. High and R. C. Wilson, Factors influencing organizational effectiveness, VII. *Personnel Psychology,* 1955, 8 (2), 245-257.

Cooley, C. H., *Social Organization* (New York: Scribner, 1909).

Cooper, William W., Harold J. Leavitt and Maynard W. Shelly II (eds.): *New Perspectives in Organization Research* (New York: John Wiley, 1964).

Cowley, W. H., The traits of face to face leaders. *Journal of Abnormal and Social Psychology,* 1931, 26, 304-313.

Crockett, Walter H., Emergent leadership in small decision-making groups. *Journal of Abnormal and Social Psychology,* 1955, 51, 378-383.

Crozier, Michael, *The Bureaucratic Phenomenon* (Chicago: The University of Chicago Press, 1964).

Cyert, Richard M., W. R. Dill, and James G. March, The role of expectations in business decision making, *Administrative Science Quarterly,* 3 (December 1958) pp. 307-340.

———, and James G. March, *A Behavioral Theory of the Firm* (Englewood Cliffs, New Jersey: Prentice-Hall, Inc., 1963).

Dale, Ernest, *The Great Organizers* (New York: McGraw-Hill Book Company, 1960).

Dalton, M., *Men Who Manage* (New York: Wiley, 1959).

Day, Robert C. and Robert L. Hamblin, Some effects of close and punitive styles of supervision. *The American Journal of Sociology,* 1964, 69, 499-510.

Dent, J. K., Managerial leadership styles: some dimensions, determinants, and behavioral correlates. Unpublished doctoral dissertation, University of Michigan, 1957.

Deutsch, Morton. An experimental study of the effects of cooperation and competition upon group process. *Human Relations,* 1949, 2, 199-231.

Dill, William R., Environment as an influence of managerial autonomy. *Administrative Science Quarterly,* 2, March, 1958, 409-443.

————, Thomas L. Hinton, and Walter R. Reitman, *The New Managers* (Englewood Cliffs, New Jersey: Prentice-Hall, Inc., 1962).

Dittes, James E., Attractiveness of group as function of self-esteem and acceptance by group. *Journal of Abnormal and Social Psychology,* 1959, 59, 77-82.

Drucker, Peter F., *Effective Executive* (New York: Harper and Row, 1967).

————, *Landmarks of Tomorrow* (New York: Harper and Row, 1959).

————, *Managing for Results* (New York: Harper and Row, 1964).

————, *The Practice of Management* (New York: Harper and Row, 1954).

Dubin, R., *Human Relations in Administration* (Englewood Cliffs, New Jersey: Prentice-Hall, 1951).

————, *et al, Leadership and Productivity* (San Francisco, Calif.: Chandler Publishing Co., 1965).

Etzioni, Amitai, *A Comparative Analysis of Complex Organizations on Power, Involvement and their Correlates* (New York: The Free Press of Glencoe, 1961).

Evan, William M., The organization-set: toward a theory of inter-organizational relations. James D. Thompson (ed.), *Approaches to Organizational Design* (Pittsburgh, Pa.: The University of Pittsburgh Press, 1966).

Evans, C. E., Supervisory responsibility and authority. *American Management Association, Reserve Report,* 30, 1957.

Festinger, Leon, Stanley Schachter and Kurt Back, *Social Pressures in Informal Groups* (New York: Harper and Row, 1950).

Fiedler, Fred E., *Leader Attitudes and Group Effectiveness* (Urbana, Ill.: Univ. of Illinois, 1958).

————, Leadership and leadership effectiveness traits: a reconceptualization of the leadership trait problem. Luigi Petrullo and Bernard M. Bass (eds.). *Leadership and Interpersonal Behavior* (New York: Holt, Rinehart and Winston, Inc., 1961).

————, *A Theory of Leadership Effectiveness* (New York: McGraw-Hill Book Company, 1967).

Fleishman, Edwin A., Leadership climate, human relations training, and supervisory behavior. *Personnel Psychology,* 1953, 6, 205-222.

————, The measurement of leadership attitudes in industry. *Journal of Applied Psychology,* 1953, 37, 153-158.

———, E. F. Harris and H. E. Burtt, Leadership and supervision in industry. *Ohio State Business Education Reserve Monograph,* 1955, 33.

———, and Edwin Harris, Patterns of leadership behavior related to employee grievances and turnover. *Personnel Psychology,* 1962, 15, 43-56.

———, and David R. Peters, Interpersonal values, leadership attitudes, and managerial "success." *Personnel Psychology,* 1962, 15, 127-143.

Foa, Uriel G., Relation of worker's expectations to satisfaction with the supervisor. *Personnel Psychology,* 1957, 10, 161-168.

Foundation for Research on Human Behavior. *Assessing Managerial Potential* (Ann Arbor, Mich.: author, 1958).

———, *Creativity and Conformity: a Problem for Organizations* (Ann Arbor, Mich.: author, 1958).

———, *Communication Problems in Superior-Subordinate Relationships* (Ann Arbor, Mich.: author, 1960).

———, *An Action Research Program for Organization Improvement* (Ann Arbor, Mich.: author, 1960).

———, *Managing Major Change in Organizations* (Ann Arbor, Mich.: 1960).

Frank, Andrew G., Goal ambiguity and conflicting standards. *Human Organization,* 17, Winter, 1958, 8-13.

French, J. R. P., Jr. A formal theory of social power. *Psychological Review,* 1956, 63 (3), 181-194.

———, J. Israel and D. Ās, An experiment on participation in a Norwegian factory. *Human Relations,* 1960, 13 (1), 3-19.

———, Jr., I. C. Ross, S. Kirby, J. R. Nelson and P. Smyth, Employee participation in a program of industrial change. *Personnel,* November-December, 1958, 16-29.

Freud, Sigmund, *The Ego and the Id* (London: Hogarth Press, 1927).

———, *New Introductory Lectures on Psychoanalysis* (New York: Norton, 1933).

Friedmann, G., *Industrial Society: The Emergency of Human Problems of Automation* (Glencoe, Ill.: Free Press, 1948).

Fromm, Eric, *The Sane Society* (New York: Rinehart, 1955).

Gardner, John W. "The Antileadership Vaccine." (Reprinted from the 1965 *Annual Report,* Carnegie Corporation of New York.) See also "Executive Trends Beat the Management Shortage" *Nation's Business,* 52, No. 9 (September, 1964).

Gaudet, Frederick J. and A. Ralph Carli, Why executives fail. *Personnel Psychology,* 1957, 10, 7-21.

Gellerman, Saul W., *Leadership Style and Employee Morale* (New York: General Electric Company, Public and Employee Relations Services, 1959).

————, *Motivation and Productivity* (New York: American Management Association, Inc., 1963).

Ghiselli, Edwin E., Individuality as a factor in the success of management personnel. *Personnel Psychology,* 1960, 13, 1-10.

————, and Barthol, R., Role perceptions of successful and unsuccessful supervisors. *Journal of Applied Psychology,* 1956, 40, 241-244.

Gibb, Cecil A., The principles and traits of leadership. *Journal of Abnormal and Social Psychology,* 1947, 42, 267-284.

————, The sociometry of leadership in temporary groups. *Sociometry,* 1950, 13, 226-243.

Goodacre, D. M., Group characteristics of good and poor performing combat units. *Sociometry,* 1953, 16 (2), 168-179.

Goodacre, Daniel M., Stimulating improved man management. *Personnel Psychology,* 1963, 16, 133-143.

Gordon, Oakley J., A factor analysis of human needs and industrial morale. *Personnel Psychology,* 1955, 8, 1-18.

Gordon, T., *Group-centered Leadership* (Boston: Houghton Mifflin, 1955).

Gore, William J., *Administrative Decision-making* (New York: John Wiley, 1964).

Green, B., Attitude measurement in G. Lindzey (ed.). *Handbook of Social Psychology* (Cambridge, Mass.: Addison-Wesley, 1954).

Greer, F. Loyal, Leader indulgence and group performance. *Psychological Monographs,* 1961, 75, No. 12, Whole No. 516.

Gross, N., W. S. Mason and A. McEachern, *Explorations in Role Analysis* (New York: John Wiley, 1958).

Gross, Neal and William E. Martin, On group cohesiveness. *American Journal of Sociology,* 1952, 57, 546-554.

Guest, Robert H., *Organizational Change: The Effect of Successful Leadership* (Homewood, Ill.: Dorsey Press and Richard D. Irwin, Inc., 1962).

Gulick, Luther and L. Urwick (eds.), *Papers on the Science of Administration* (New York: Institute of Public Administration, 1937).

Haire, M., *Psychology in Management* (New York: McGraw-Hill, 1956).

Halpin, Andrew W., *The Leadership Behavior of School Superintendents* (Chicago: Midwest Administration Center, The University of Chicago, 1959).

Hamblin, Robert L., Leadership and crises. In *Group Dynamics: Research and Theory* (2nd ed.) Dorwin Cartwright and Alvin Zander (eds.). Evanston, Ill.: Row, Peterson and Company, 1960. (Also in *Sociometry,* 1958, 21, 322-335.)

Hammond, Leo K. and Morton Goldman, Competition and non-competition and its relationship to individual and group productivity. *Sociometry,* 1961, 24, 46-60.

Haney, William H., *Communication and Organizational Behavior Text and Cases*, Revised Edition (Homewood, Ill.: Richard D. Irwin, Inc., 1967).

Harary, F., and R. Norman, *Graph Theory as a Mathematical Model in the Social Sciences* (Ann Arbor, Mich.: Institute for Social Research, 1953).

Hare, A. Paul, *Handbook of Small Group Research* (New York: Free Press of Glencoe, Inc., 1962).

————, E. F. Borgatta and R. F. Bales, *Small Groups* (New York: Knopf, 1955).

Healey, James H., Coordination and control of executive functions. *Personnel*, 1956, 33, 106-117.

Hemphill, John K., Relations between the size of the group and the behavior of "superior" leaders. *The Journal of Social Psychology*, 1950, 32, 11-32.

————, Why people attempt to lead. In *Leadership and Interpersonal Behavior*, Luigi Petrullo and Bernard M. Bass (eds.) (New York: Holt, Rinehart and Winston, Inc., 1961).

————, and Alvin E. Coons, Development of the leader behavior description and questionnaire. In *Leader Behavior: Its Description and Measurement*, Ralph M. Stogdill and Alvin E. Coons (eds.) (Columbus, Ohio: Ohio State University, Bureau of Business Research, Monograph No. 88, 1957).

Herzberg, Frederick, *Work and the Nature of Man* (New York: World Publishing Co., 1966).

Herzberg, F., B. Mausner and Barbara Snyderman, *The Motivation to Work* (2nd ed.) (New York: Wiley, 1959).

Hollander, E. P., Emergent leadership and social influence. In *Leadership and Interpersonal Behavior*, Luigi Petrullo and Barnard M. Bass (eds.) (New York: Holt, Rinehart and Winston, Inc., 1961.)

Homans, G. C., *The Human Group* (New York: Harcourt, Brace and World, 1950).

Hoppock, R., *Job Satisfaction* (New York: Harper, 1935).

Horsfall, A. B., and C. M. Arensberg. Teamwork and productivity in a shoe factory. *Human Organization*, 1949, 8, 13-25.

Houser, J. D., What People Want from Business (New York: McGraw-Hill, 1938).

Hovland, C. I., I. L. Janis, and H. H. Kelley, *Communication and Persuasion* (New Haven, Conn.: Yale Univer., 1953).

————, and I. L. Janis (eds.), *Personality and Persuasibility*, 2, Yale Studies in Attitude and Communication (New Haven, Conn.: Yale Univer., 1959).

Hovland, C. I., and M. J. Roseberg, *Attitude, Organization and Change*, 3, Yale Studies in Attitude and Communication (New Haven, Conn.: Yale Univer., 1960).

Hughes, Everett C., *Men and their Work* (New York: The Free Press of Glencoe, 1958).

Hyman, Herbert H., The psychology of status. *Archives of Psychology*, 269, 1942.

Indik, Bernard P., Basil S. Georgopoulos and Stanley E. Seashore, Superior subordinate relationships and performance. *Personnel Psychology*, 1961, 14, 357-374.

Institute for Social Research. *Factors Related to Productivity* (Ann Arbor, Mich.: author, 1951).

Jackson, J. M., The effect of changing the leadership of small work groups. *Human Relations*, 1953, 6 (1), 25-44.

——, and H. D. Saltzstein, *Group Membership and Group Conformity Processes* (Ann Arbor, Mich.: Institute for Social Research, 1956).

James, William, *The Principles of Psychology* Vol. 1 (London: Macmillan and Co., Ltd., 1890).

Janowitz, Morris, Changing patterns of organizational authority: the military establishment. *Administrative Science Quarterly*, 3, March, 1959, 473-493.

Jaques, E., *The Changing Culture of a Factory* (London: Tavistock Publications, 1951).

——, *Measurement of Responsibility* (London: Tavistock Publications, 1956).

Jenkins, W. O., A review of leadership studies with particular reference to military problems. *Psychological Bulletin*, 1947, 44 (1) 54-79.

Jennings, Eugene E., The anatomy of leadership. *Management of Personnel Quarterly*, I (1) (Autumn, 1961).

Kahn, R. L., Human relations on the shop floor. E. M. Hugh-Jones (ed.), *Human Relations and Modern Management* (Amsterdam: North-Holland Publishing Co., 1958, pp. 43-74).

——, The prediction of productivity. *Journal of Social Issues*, 1956, 12 (2), 41-49.

——, Productivity and job satisfaction. *Personnel Psychology*, 1960, 13 (3), 275-278.

——, and D. Katz, Leadership practices in relation to productivity and morale. D. Cartwright and A. Zander (eds.), *Group Dynamics: Research and Theory* (2nd ed.) (Evanston, Ill.: Row, Peterson, 1960, 554-571).

Katz, D., Morale and motivation in industry. In W. Dennis (ed.), *Current Trends in Industrial Psychology* (Pittsburgh: Univer. of Pittsburgh, 1949, 145-171).

——, N. Maccoby, G. Gurin and L. G. Floor, *Productivity, Supervision and Morale Among Railroad Workers* (Ann Arbor, Mich.: Institute for Social Research, 1951).

————, ————, and Nancy Morse, *Productivity, Supervision and Morale in an Office Situation* (Ann Arbor, Mich.: Institute for Social Research, 1950).

Kepner, C. H., and B. B. Tregoe, *The Rational Manager* (New York: McGraw-Hill, 1965).

Knickerbocker, Irving, Leadership: a conception and some implications. *The Journal of Social Issues,* 1948, 4 (3), 23-40.

Koontz, Harold, and Cyril O'Donnel, *Principles of Management,* 2nd edition (New York: McGraw-Hill Book Company, Inc., 1959).

Korman, A. K., " 'Consideration,' 'Initiating Structure,' and Organizational Criteria—A Review," *Personnel Psychology: A Journal of Applied Research,* 19 (4), 349-361.

Krulee, G. K., The Scanlon plan: co-operation through participation. *Journal of Business,* University of Chicago, 1955, 28 (2), 100-113.

Leavitt, H. J., *Managerial Psychology* (Chicago: University of Chicago, 1958).

Lewin, K., *Field Theory in Social Science.* D. Cartwright (ed.) (New York: Harper, 1951).

————, Frontiers in group dynamics. *Human Relations,* 1947, 1, 5-41.

————, Group decision and social change. E. E. Maccoby, T. M. Newcomb, and E. L. Hartley (eds.), *Readings in Social Psychology* (3rd ed.) (New York: Holt, Rinehart and Winston, 1958, 197-211).

————, *Resolving Social Conflict* (Gertrude Lewin, ed.) (New York: Harper, 1948).

————, R. Lippitt and R. White, "Leader Behavior and Member Reaction in Three 'Social Climates' " in Cartwright and Zander (eds.), *Group Dynamics.*

Lieberman, S., The effects of changes in roles on the attitudes of role occupants. *Human Relations,* 1956, 9 (4), 385-402.

Likert, Rensis, Effective supervision: an adaptive and relative process. *Personnel Psychology,* 1958, II (3), 317-352.

————, *The Human Organization* (New York: McGraw-Hill Book Co., 1967).

————, Measuring organizational performance. *Harvard Business Review,* 1958, 36 (2), 41-50.

————, Motivational approach to management development. *Harvard Business Review,* 1959, 37 (4), 75-82.

————, Motivation: the core of management. American Management Association, *Personnel Series* (155), 1953, 3-21.

————, *New Patterns of Management* (New York: McGraw-Hill Book Company, Inc., 1961).

————, and D. Katz, Supervisory practices and organizational structures as they affect employee productivity and morale. American Management Association, *Personnel Series* (120), 1948, 14-24.

Lippitt, R., and L. Bradford, Role-playing in supervisory training. *Personnel,* 1946, 22, 3-14.

———, Jeanne Watson and B. Westley, *The Dynamics of Planned Change: A Comparative Study of Principles and Techniques* (New York: Harcourt, Brace and World, 1958).

Litterer, J. A., *Analysis of Organizations* (New York: John Wiley, 1965).

McClelland, David C., *Personality* (New York: Holt, Rinehart, and Winston, 1951).

———, *Studies in Motivation* (New York: Appleton-Century Crofts Publishing Co., 1955).

———, et al., *The Achievement Motive* (New York: Appleton-Century Crofts, Inc., 1953).

———, et al., *The Achieving Society* (Princeton, New Jersey: D. Van Nostrand Co., 1961).

McGregor, Douglas, Conditions of effective leadership in industrial organization. *Journal of Consulting Psychologists,* 1944, 8, 56-63.

———, *Human Side of Enterprise* (New York: McGraw-Hill, 1960).

———, *Leadership and Motivation* (Boston: MIT Press, 1966).

———, *Professional Manager* (New York: McGraw-Hill, 1967).

McMurry, R. N., The case for benevolent autocracy. *Harvard Business Review,* 1958, 36, 82-90.

Maier, N. R. F., *Psychology in Industry* (2nd ed.) (New York: Houghton Mifflin, 1955).

Mailick, Sidney and Edward H. Van Ness, *Concepts and Issues in Administrative Behavior* (Englewood Cliffs, New Jersey: Prentice-Hall, Inc., 1962).

Mann, F. C., Changing superior-subordinate relationships. *Journal of Social Issues,* 1951, 7 (3), 56-63.

———, Putting human relations research findings to work. *Michigan Business Review,* 1950, 2 (2), 16-20.

———, Studying and creating change: a means of understanding social organization. *Research in Industrial Human Relations* (Madison, Wis.: Industrial Relations Research Asso., 1957, 146-167.

———, and L. R. Hoffman, *Automation and the Worker: a Study of Social Change in Power Plants* (New York: Holt, Rinehart and Winston, 1960).

March, J. G., and H. A. Simon, *Organizations* (New York: Wiley, 1958.

Marcus, Philip M., Supervision and group process. *Human Organization,* 1961, 20 (1), 15-19.

Marrow, A. J., D. G. Bowers, and S. E. Seashore (eds.), *Strategies of Organizational Change* (New York: Harper and Row, 1967).

Maslow, Abraham H., *Eupsychian, Management* (Homewood, Ill.: Richard D. Irwin, and The Dorsey Press, 1965).

———, *Motivation and Personality* (New York: Harper and Row, 1954).

———, *New Knowledge in Human Values* (Scranton, Pa.: Harper and Row, 1959).

———, *Toward a Psychology of Being* (Princeton, New Jersey: Van Nostrand Publishing Co., 1962).

Mayo, Elton, *The Human Problems of an Industrial Civilization* (New York: The Macmillan Company, 1933).

———, *The Social Problems of an Industrial Civilization* (Cambridge, Mass.: Harvard Univer., 1945).

Medalia, Nahum Z., Unit size and leadership perception. *Sociometry,* 1954, 17, 64-67.

———, Delbert C. Miller, Human relations leadership and the association of morale and efficiency in work groups. *Social Forces,* 1955, 33, 348-352.

Mellinger, G. D., Interpersonal trust as a factor in communication. *Journal of Abnormal and Social Psychology,* 1956, 52 (3), 304-309.

Meltzer, Leo and James Salter, Organizational structure and performance job satisfaction. *American Sociological Review,* 1962, 27, 351-362.

Milgram, Stanley, Group pressure and action against a person. *Journal of Abnormal and Social Psychology,* 1964, 69, 137-143.

Miller, J. G., Toward a general theory for the behavioral sciences. *American Psychologist,* 1955, 10, 513-531.

Miller, Walter B., Two concepts of authority. *American Anthropologist,* 57 (April, 1955), 271-289.

Miner, John B., and John E. Culver, Some aspects of the executive personality. *Journal of Applied Psychology,* 1955, 39, 348-353.

Morse, Nancy and R. Weiss, The function and meaning of work and the job. *American Social Review,* 1955, 20 (2), 191-198.

Nagle, Bryant F., Productivity, employee attitude and supervisor sensitivity. *Personnel Psychology,* 1954, 7, 219-233.

National Training Laboratories. *Explorations in Human Relations Training* (Washington: National Education Association, 1953).

Newcomb, T. M., *Social Psychology* (New York: Holt, Rinehart and Winston, 1950).

Newman, William H., and Charles E. Summer, *The Process of Management* (Englewood Cliffs, New Jersey: Prentice-Hall, Inc., 1961).

Oaklander, Harold, and Edwin A. Fleishman, Patterns of leadership related to organizational stress in hospital settings. *Administrative Science Quarterly,* 1964, 8, 520-532.

Obrochta, Richard J., Foreman-worker attitude patterns. *Journal of Applied Psychology,* 1960, 44, 88-91.

Odiorne, George S., *Management by Objectives* (New York: Pitman Publishing Corporation, 1965).

O'Donnell, C., The source of managerial authority. *Political Science Quarterly*, 1952, 67, 573.

Packard, Vance. *The Status Seekers* (New York: David McKay Company, 1959).

Parker, T. C., Relationships among measures of supervisory behavior, group behavior, and situational characteristics. *Personnel Psychology*, 1963, 16, 319-334.

Patchen, M., The effect of reference group standards on job satisfactions. *Human Relations*, 1958, 11 (4), 303-314.

Pearlin, Leonard I., Sources of resistance to change in a mental hospital. *American Journal of Sociology*, 1962, 68, 325-334.

Pelz, D. C., Influence: a key to effective leadership in the first-line supervisor. *Personnel*, November, 1952, 3-11.

————, Leadership within a hierarchial organization. *Journal of Social Issues*, 7, 1951, 49-55.

————, Motivation of the engineering and research specialist. American Management Association, *General Management Series*, 186, 1957, 25-46.

————, Some social factors related to performance in a research organization. *Administrative Science Quarterly*, 1956, 1 (3), 310-325.

Peres, Sherwood H., Performance dimensions of supervisory positions. *Personnel Psychology*, 1962, 15, 405-410.

Perrow, Charles, The analysis of goals in complex organizations. *American Sociological Review*, 26 (December, 1961), 854-866.

Pfiffner, J. M., The effective supervisor: an organization research study. *Personnel*, 1955, 31, 530-540.

Porter, Donald E., and Philip B. Applewhite, *Studies in Organizational Behavior and Management* (Scranton, Pa.: International Textbook Company, 1964).

Porter, Lyman W., A study of perceived need satisfactions in bottom and middle management jobs. *Journal of Applied Psychology*, 1961, 45, 1-10.

Pryer, Margaret W., Austin W. Flint, and Bernard M. Bass, Group effectiveness and consistency of leadership. *Sociometry*, 1962, 25, 391-397.

Reid, P., Supervision in an automated plant. *Supervisory Management* (August, 1960), 2-10.

Reisman, David, *The Lonely Crowd* (New Haven, Conn.: Yale University Press, 1950).

Revans, R. W., The analysis of industrial behavior. *Automatic Production-change and Control* (London: Institution of Production Engineering, 1957).

Rice, A. K., *Productivity and Social Organization* (London: Tavistock Publications, 1958).

Roach, Darrell E., Factor analysis of rated supervisory behavior. *Personnel Psychology*, 1956, 9, 487-498.

Roethlisberger, F. J., *Management and Morale* (Cambridge, Mass.: Harvard Univer., 1941).

————, and W. J. Dickson, *Management and the Worker* (Cambridge, Mass.: Harvard Univer. Press, 1939).

Rogers, C. R., *Counseling and Psychotherapy* (Boston: Houghton Mifflin, 1942).

Ronken, H. O., and P. R. Lawrence, *Administering Changes* (Boston: Harvard Graduate School of Business Administration, 1952).

Ross, I. C., and A. Zander, Need satisfactions and employee turnover. *Personnel Psychology*, 1957, 10 (3), 327-338.

Rubenstein, Albert H., and Chadwick J. Haberstroh, *Some Theories of Organization* (Homewood, Ill.: Richard D. Irwin, Inc., 1960).

Sanford, Fillmore H., *Authoritarianism and Leadership* (Philadelphia: Institute for Research in Human Relations, 1950).

————, Leadership identification and acceptance. *Groups, Leadership and Men*, Harold Guetzkow (ed.) (Pittsburgh: Carnegie Press, 1951).

Schachter, Stanley, *The Psychology of Affiliation* (Stanford, Calif.: Stanford University Press, 1959).

Schaffer, R. H., Job satisfaction as related to need satisfaction in work. *Psychological Monographs*, 1953, 67, No. 14.

Schein, E. H., and W. C. Bennis, *Personal and Organizational Change Through Group Methods* (New York: John Wiley, 1965).

Schleh, E. C., *Management by Results* (New York: McGraw-Hill, 1961).

Selznick, P., *Leadership in Administration* (Evanston, Ill.: Row, Peterson, 1957).

Shartle, C. L., *Effective Performance and Leadership* (Englewood Cliffs, New Jersey: Prentice-Hall, 1956).

Shultz, G. P., Worker participation on production problems. American Management Association, *Personnel*, 1951, 28 (3), 202-211.

Simon, H. A., *Administrative Behavior* (New York: Macmillan, 1947).

————, *Models of Man, Social and Rational* (New York: John Wiley, Inc., 1957).

Spector, Aaron J., Expectations, fulfillment, and morale. *Journal of Abnormal and Social Psychology*, 1956, 52, 51-56.

Stagner, Ross, Motivational aspects of industrial morale. *Personnel Psychology*, 1958, 11, 64-70.

————, Psychological aspects of industrial conflict: perception. *Personnel Psychology*, 1948, 1, 131-143.

Stanton, Erwin S., Company policies and supervisors' attitudes toward supervision. *Journal of Applied Psychology*, 1960, 44, 22-26.

Steiner, Ivan D., and Homer H. Johnson, Authoritarianism and conformity. *Sociometry*, 1963, 26, 21-34.

Stewart, Michael, Resistance to technological change in industry. *Human Organization*, 1957, 16 (3), 36-39.

Stogdill, R. M., *Individual Behavior and Group Achievement* (New York: Oxford Press, 1959).

——, and C. L. Shartle, *Methods in the Study of Administrative Leadership* (Columbus, Ohio: Ohio State University, Bureau of Business Research, 1956).

——, *Patterns of Administrative Performance* (Columbus, Ohio: Ohio State University, Bureau of Business Research, 1956).

Suojanen, Waino W., The span of control—fact or fable? *Advanced Management*, 1955, 20 (11), 5-13. *The Dynamics of Management* (New York: Holt, Rinehart and Winston, 1966).

Sutermeister, Robert A., *People and Productivity* (New York: McGraw-Hill Book Company, 1963).

Talacchi, Sergio, Organization size, individual attitudes and behavior. *Administrative Science Quarterly*, 1960, 5, 398-420.

Tannenbaum, A. S., The concept of organizational control. *Journal of Social Issues*, 1956, 12 (2), 50-60.

——, Personality change as a result of an experimental change of environmental conditions. *Journal of Abnormal Social Psychology*, 1957, 52, 404-406.

——, and F. H. Allport, Personality structure and group structure: an interpretative study of their relationship through an event-structure hypothesis. *Journal of Abnormal Social Psychology*, 1956, 51 (3), 272-280.

Tannenbaum, Robert, and Schmidt, Warren H., How to choose a leadership pattern. *Harvard Business Review* (March-April, 1958), 95-102.

——, Irving R. Weschler, and Massarik, *Leadership and Organization: A Behavioral Science Approach* (New York: McGraw-Hill Book Company, Inc., 1959).

Taylor, Frederick W., *Scientific Management* (New York: Harper and Row, 1911).

Terry, George R., *Principles of Management*, 3rd ed. (Homewood, Ill.: Richard D. Irwin, Inc., 1960).

Thelen, H. A., *Dynamics of Groups at Work* (Chicago: University of Chicago, 1954).

Thibaut, John W., and Harold H. Kelley, *The Social Psychology of Groups* (New York: John Wiley and Sons, Inc., 1959).

Thomas, Edwin J., Role concepts and organizational size. *American Sociological Review*, 24 (February, 1959), 30-37.

Thompson, James D., Common and uncommon elements in administration. *The Social Welfare Forum* (New York: Columbia University Press, 1962).

————, and Frederick L. Bates, Technology, organization, and administration. *Administrative Science Quarterly*, 2 (December, 1957), 325-342.

————, and William J. McEwen, Organizational goals and environment: goal-setting as an interaction process, *American Sociological Review*, 23 (February, 1958), 23-31.

Trow, Donald B., Autonomy and job satisfaction to task oriented groups. *Journal of Abnormal and Social Psychology*, 1957, 54, 204-209.

Trumbo, Don A., Individual and group correlates of attitudes toward work-related change. *Journal of Applied Psychology*, 1961, 45, 338-344.

Turner, Arthur N., Interaction and sentiment in the foreman-worker relationship. *Human Organization*, 1955, 14 (1), 10-16.

Viteles, M. S., *Motivation and Morale in Industry* (New York: Norton, 1953).

Vroom, V. H., The effects of attitudes on the perception of organizational goals. *Human Relations*, 1960, 13 (3), 229-240.

————, Employee attitudes. In R. Gray (ed.), *Frontiers of Industrial Relations* (Pasadena, Calif.: California Institute of Technology, 1960).

————, *Some Personality Determinants of the Effects of Participation* (Englewood Cliffs, New Jersey: Prentice-Hall, 1960).

————, and F. C. Mann, Leader authoritarianism and employee attitudes. *Personnel Psychology*, 1960, 13 (2), 125-140.

Walker, C., and H. Guest, *The Man on the Assembly Line* (Cambridge, Mass.: Harvard University Press, 1952).

Weitz, Joseph and Nuckols, Robert C., Job satisfaction and job survival. *Journal of Applied Psychology*, 1955, 39, 294-300.

Westerlund, G., *Group Leadership and Field Experiment* (Stockholm: Nordisk Rotogravyr, 1952).

White, Harrison, "Management Conflict and Sociometric Structure," *American Journal of Sociology*, Vol. 67, September, 1961, 185-199.

White, Robert W., and R. Lippitt, *Autocracy and Democracy: An Experimental Inquiry* (New York: Harper, 1960).

————, Motivation reconsidered: the concept of competence, *Psychological Review*, 66, 5, 1959.

Whyte, William F., Human relations theory—a progress report. *Harvard Business Review*, 1956, 34 (5), 125-134.

————, *Man and Organization* (Homewood, Ill.: Irwin Book Co., 1959).

———— (ed.), *Money and Motivation* (New York: Harper and Row, 1955).

Whyte, W. H., Jr., *The Organization Man* (New York: Simon and Schuster, 1956).

Zaleznik, A., *Worker Satisfaction and Development* (Boston: Harvard Business School, 1956).

Zander, A., E. J. Thomas, and T. Natsoulas, Personal goals and the group's goals for the member. *Human Relations*, 1960, 13 (4), 333-344.

Index